Prof. Clement's copy.

EUROPE, PARLIAMENT AND THE MEDIA

Edited by
Dr Martyn Bond

THE FEDERAL TRUST
for education & research

This book is published by the Federal Trust, whose aim is to enlighten public debate on federal issues of national, continental and global governance. It does this in the light of its statutes which state that it shall promote 'studies in the principles of international relations, international justice and supranational government.'

The Federal Trust conducts enquiries, promotes seminars and conferences and publishes reports and teaching materials. It is the UK member of the Trans-European Policy Studies Association (TEPSA), a grouping of fifteen think-tanks from member states of the European Union.

Up-to-date information about the Federal Trust can be found on the internet at www.fedtrust.co.uk

© The Federal Trust for Education and Research 2003

ISBN 1 903403 22 7

We are grateful to the London Office of the European Parliament for supporting the publication of this book.

NOTE: All contributors to this volume are writing in a personal capacity. Views expressed are those of the authors and do not represent the position of their institution.

This book is the fifth title in the Federal Trust series *Future of European Parliamentary Democracy*. The other volumes are available from the publisher: *Seven Theorems in Search of the European Parliament* (1999, 0 901573 70 1) by David Coombes; *What Next for the European Parliament* (1999, 0 901573 90 6) by Andreas Mauer, *Shaping Europe: Reflections of Three MEPs* (2000, 0 901573 99 X) by Lord Plumb, Carole Tongue and Florus Wijsenbeek; *Choice and Representation in the European Union* (2003, 0 901573 73 6) edited by Roger Morgan and Michael Steed; and *The Convention on the Future of Europe: Working Towards an EU Constitution* (1 903403 60 X) by Jo Shaw, Paul Magnette, Lars Hoffmann and Anna Vergés Bausili.

The Federal Trust is a Registered Charity No. 272241
7 Graphite Square, Vauxhall Walk,
London SE11 5EE
Company Limited by Guarantee No.1269848

Marketing and Distribution by Kogan Page Ltd
Printed by J W Arrowsmith Ltd

Contents

Preface 7
by Pat Cox, President of the European Parliament

Introduction 9
Dr Martyn Bond

Transnational television in Europe: Affluence
without influence 13
Dr Jean K. Chalaby

A Structural Bias against Pan-European TV? 31
Stewart Purvis

Media Coverage of the European Union 35
Prof David Morgan

British Press Coverage of Europe 55
Jim Dougal

Priorities in Information Policy 63
Roy Perry MEP

The (Non-)coverage of the European Parliament 77
Olivier Basnée

Media and the European Parliament
During the Convention 105
Lars Hoffmann

E-Coverage of Europe 115
Stephen Coleman and Bridie Nathanson

The Council, the media and the public at large 133
Norbert Schwaiger

EbS: the Commission's flagship 157
Anthony O'Donnell

The European Parliament and the Media 167
Jean-Charles Pierron

Media and Mobilization in the 1999 European Parliamentary
    Election 189
Susan A. Banducci and Holli Semetko

Notes on Contributors 205

Preface
by Pat Cox,
President of the European Parliament

Europe is a political reality, and has been so for many years. Each European treaty adds to the relevance and the authority of the Institutions that govern the European Union. And yet in many countries there seems a strange disjuncture between this legal and political reality and the popular perception of Europe.

European politicians strive to make the Union and its activities as relevant to the electorate as possible, and yet the turnout at successive European elections has fallen. National governments strive to gain credit for the successes they achieve in European negotiations, and yet electorates grow more and more sceptical of their involvement in the European Union. The disjuncture is becoming patent, and political leaders at the highest level are seriously concerned with the growing disenchantment of the public with politics generally, and specifically with politics at the European level.

What role does the media play in this? Does it do no more than reflect popular disenchantment, or is it the cause itself of distrust between the governed and the governing class? How far can the media in this diverse and variegated continent of Europe contribute to a better understanding of the issues at stake for all of us?

If there were easy answers we would have found them by now. This collection of essays – by commentators, academics, journalists, civil servants and politicians themselves – does not pretend to offer a magic solution, a panacea to cure the political sickness. But it does push the diagnosis further, examining practical constraints in the television market, for instance, as well as policy options in the political sphere. It gives plenty of food for thought for anyone concerned with the mismatch between the growing importance of Europe, and of the European Parliament in particular, and the low saliency in public opinion and weak support for the European project on the other.

These issues need to be thought through, discussed and eventually put right. This book offers a small step in that direction. It will help all readers think through the issues more clearly.

Introduction
Dr Martyn Bond

These essays relate to three interlocking themes: popular perceptions of Europe, public participation in politics, and the role of the media. They touch on wider issues such as the declining attractiveness of representational democracy in contemporary society and the constraints imposed – some might say the opportunities offered – by modern technological advances affecting the media. But central to the focus of the book is the European Parliament, since this embodies perhaps more clearly than the other Institutions the democratic paradox. At the very same time that the public is expressing its hesitation through declining voter turnout at European elections, the European Parliament is gaining more and more powers and responsibilities.

The essays look at the issues from different perspectives. Jean Chalaby considers the development of transnational television in Europe, highlighting the difficulties experienced by various initiatives whose early confidence in the prospect of large audiences across national and linguistic borders has largely been disappointed. Stewart Purvis confirms this academic analysis through his professional experience of running Euronews, the multilingual trans-european TV station with which he was intimately involved for several years as CEO of ITN. His comments on the distinction between commercial and public service requirements in this field carry the authority of someone who has actually had day-to-day responsibility for transmitting programmes that Europeans are invited to watch.

Professor Morgan reviews the field of media coverage of the European Union, contrasting two examples: the BSE crisis of 1996 and the European Elections of 1999. He sets these examples against a backdrop of the changing political and media context of European coverage in Britain during the last twenty years. His conclusions spare neither the press nor the broadcasters, and paint a picture of an increasingly competitive struggle for news management by member state governments as well as the European Institutions. Jim Dougall's energetic critique of British press coverage confirms these findings and shows the extent of the problem of changing popular perceptions in this country as far as the European Institutions are concerned.

Roy Perry MEP speaks with the authority of an elected representative who has held responsibility in the European Parliament for overseeing the information policy of the European Union. He is clearly not impressed by the results of what he has seen and his comments are sharp. His critique is that of an insider and all the more valuable for that, since he puts his finger on some of the weaknesses of a bureaucratic system that enters the fray with the media both as a subject and as an object. Being less than a government – and considerably less coherent as well – the Institutions are inevitably in a weaker position than national actors, and their performance appears to confirm his worst fears.

Looking at the nature of reporting at the heart of the system, Olivier Basnée sheds some light on the distinctions between national journalistic traditions – in particular between the British and the French – among the press corps in Brussels. But the distinctions are not only between nations; they are also between different types of journalism, one which he finds collusive with the Institutions, very closely bound up with the creation of the European project, and another which he identifies as investigative and critical. In this the Parliament has probably suffered more from the latter while the Commission has probably benefited more from the former. But the Convention on the Future of Europe, which led to the draft Constitution, offered the European Parliament an opportunity to improve its profile. Through its experienced and well prepared delegates, Parliament managed to take the initiative and guide the Convention in many areas. Its image consequently improved, as Lars Hoffman's insightful essay illustrates.

But one swallow surely does not make a summer, and the temporary respite afforded by more positive coverage of Parliament during the Convention does not indicate a reversal of the general trend towards public neglect of representative political institutions. Professor Stephen Coleman and Bridie Nathanson illustrate this clearly in their practical survey of e-democracy. New developments in technology certainly have a role to play in stemming the tide of public disinterest, but they argue that they must be placed within wider strategies for re-invigorating democracy, both formal and informal. Their list of recommendations is long, but any serious effort to grapple with the problem will need to assess carefully the value of each of their recommendations.

Within the European Institutions themselves there has been much soul searching and many practical initiatives to try to relate the European experiment more closely to the citizen. That is particularly true since the near failure of the referendum on the Treaty of Maastricht in France. Norbert Schwaiger, who writes against the background of a lifetime's professional involvement in these issues from within the Council of Ministers, demonstrates with clarity the steps that have been taken there to open that most secretive of Institutions to greater public scrutiny. Starting from the traditional position of the Council as the arbiter of intergovernmental diplomacy, he goes on to describe how a commitment to transparency – both in access to documents and in media presence at meetings – has over a relatively small number of years transformed to working atmosphere of the Secretariat .

One of the most important tools for increasing public awareness of what is going on in Europe is a dedicated television channel. To some extent Europe is following American experience in this field, where an independent cable channel dedicated initially to Congressional affairs and subsequently to wider political events has been in operation for thirty years. *Europe by Satellite*, the management of which is entrusted to the Commission, is the Brussels equivalent – in different circumstances – to Washington's *C-Span*. Rather than limit EBS to coverage of the European Parliament, it began with a wider brief than its American equivalent and broadcast to other broadcasters rather than direct to the public. Though the credibility of the channel may have suffered somewhat through the initial decision to vest responsibility in the Commission whose business it was also covering, take-up of EBS by other channels has grown strongly over the years. As Tony O'Donnell's article makes clear, it well fulfils its objective of offering to TV stations for re-broadcasting a considerable volume of material regarding European political events that they could not obtain otherwise.

In his article on TV and radio coverage of the European Parliament Jean Pierron, who has been responsible for the audio-visual division of Parliament for some fifteen years, demonstrates with facts and figures the extent both of direct coverage and of indirect encouragement of broadcast journalists to report on Parliament and its activities. The record is strongly positive, highlighting the paradox of falling turn-out at elections despite such efforts at media support.

Susan Banducci and Holli Semetko survey the media environment in which information about the European Parliament, and in particular about European elections, is disseminated. Their research throws up fascinating disparities of exposure country by country, both in broadcast media and in the written press, and they go on to analyse the content of coverage specifically for the 1999 elections. The purpose of their work is to trace just who is mobilized by exposure to information about the issues raised during the election campaign. They do not come to a single conclusion, but they raise the provocative thought that more information may not in all cases lead to greater public involvement.

So the range of these articles is wide and the concerns covered are kaleidoscopic. Some of these essays are strongly pro-active and educationally oriented, aiming to encourage instruction of the public on matters political and European. Others are more reticent, more academic, eschewing any approach which might smack of propaganda, rather leaving the field open for the free-for-all of conflicting opinion. The European project is for them not something that can be delivered by media policy, however well designed and efficiently executed. All of them recognise the need for further analysis and discussion, and some call for more action, to stem the tide of political discontent. They identify problems and, where possible, suggest solutions. Whether journalists, civil servants, politicians or academics, all are concerned to improve the quality of European democracy.

Transnational television in Europe: Affluence without influence
Dr Jean K. Chalaby

Introduction

My aim in writing this article is twofold. First, I want to retrace the history of trans-border TV channels since the beginning of satellite television in Europe in 1982. During an initial period, international channels faced seemingly insurmountable technological, economic and programming difficulties. Satellite technology was in its infancy, too few households subscribed to cable networks and those who did had access to international programming that was unadapted to their tastes. The decade witnessed many casualties and most ventures had a short life span.

The prospects of the industry improved in the mid-1990s. The fast increase of homes having access and subscribing to satellite and cable television services expanded the reception universe of transnational channels, alongside the collapse of communism in Central and Eastern Europe, which opened out new markets eastwards. Communication satellites became more powerful, capable of carrying many more channels and delivering them directly to viewers, heralding the era of direct-to-home broadcasting. The European directive Television Without Frontiers removed any lingering national barriers to the international transmission of TV signals.

Second I suggest that the expansion of transnational TV channels has had little impact on the formation of a European public sphere. The key to the success of many of these channels is their ability to adjust to European cultural diversity. As networks of local channels replace international feeds, few cross-border channels remain that have not divided the multinational market into distinct audiences. Those that have kept a commitment to the concept of a transnational public usually sell international news to the business and political elite. The European TV market has not adjusted to the development of cross-border governance in Europe, raising issues about the participatory nature of transnational democracy in the region.

The Development of transnational television in Europe

From the early 1980s to the early 1990s, the emergent international broadcasters found the shift from a national to an international context more difficult than they had foreseen. The fledgling industry was in the grip of a series of problems that included poor satellite transmissions, expensive home reception equipment, governments reluctant to grant access to their market, and a reception universe that was too small to attract advertisers and cover costs. It was also searching for a workable model of international broadcasting and a suitable way of addressing a multinational audience. It was struggling with issues regarding programme production, scheduling, marketing, presentation and a whole range of linguistic problems from translation to multi-lingual television services (Barrand 1986, p.11). Facing such difficulties, many of the early cross-border channels were ventures of short duration, either disappearing altogether or re-launched in a new format by a new proprietor.

The first satellite channel was launched in April 1982 and operated under the name of Satellite Television, after the company that launched it, transmitting from the OTS, Eutelsat's first communications satellite. By 1983, the company was bought by Rupert Murdoch who was keen to take his press empire into new directions (Tallantire 1994). He renamed it Sky Channel and in order to increase viewing on the continent he promptly developed an international programme schedule including shows from Germany, Belgium and the Netherlands. By 1987, more than half of Sky's programming was of European origin (Collins 1992, p. 83). Despite reaching a record 15 million homes across Europe the following year, the channel was accumulating debts and the media mogul was forced to scale down his European ambitions. In June, he abruptly pulled back from Europe and retracted Sky to the British market (Tallantire, 1989).

As Murdoch was about to leave the pan-European market, the ITV franchise holders (with the exception of Thames Television), in partnership with Richard Branson, launched Super Channel to European audiences on 30 January 1987. The channel was intended to be a showcase for ITV programming but soon ran into trouble when it became clear that English language programmes were not as popular as expected with European audiences (*Cable and Satellite Europe* June 1988, p. 63). The channel modified its plans and introduced German and Dutch programming, only to further confuse viewers. Constant meddling with the schedule prevented Super Channel from building an audience, attracting advertisers and turning a profit (Collins 1992, pp.86-8). The ITV companies pulled out of the channel in March 1988, which was progressively phased out by successive owners.

Among the cross-border channels launched in the 1980s and early 1990s, approximately 15 did not last more than a few years (*Cable and Satellite Europe* January 1994, p. 40). The satellite technology attracted newcomers such as British Telecom and WH Smith who treated international television as their entry ticket into the broadcasting industry. Their channels, which included WH Smith's Lifestyle and British Telecom's Star Channel, never found an audience and closed down following heavy losses. Among the other ill-fated ventures were TEN – The Entertainment Network (1984-1985), Robert Maxwell's Mirror Vision and Premiere (1986 to 1989), and the Arts Channel (1988) (*Cable and Satellite Europe* January 1990, p.18).

The development of satellite television was a mixed blessing for public service broadcasters. In the 1980s, they were adjusting to the recent emergence of commercial rivals following the break-up of state broadcasting monopolies in several European countries. On the one hand, satellite technology was being recognized as an exciting new medium that would provide an opportunity to disseminate the 'best' of European television to the 'widest possible European audience' (Clarke 1982, p.44). It was also perceived as a fresh threat to their position, fearing in particular that the technology would allow commercial broadcasters to re-write industry standards (Barrand 1986, p.11). Thus the early interest of public service broadcasters in satellite technology was prompted by their enthusiasm for a new technology as well as their concerns about the competition from the commercial sector.

The current doyen of transnational TV channels in Europe is the francophone TV5, which was launched in 1984 by five public television channels from France, Belgium and Switzerland. 3SAT quickly followed, which was launched by three public broadcasters from Germany (ZDF), Austria (ORF) and German-speaking Switzerland (SRG) in December of that year.

Public broadcasters' most ambitious projects were organised under the auspices of the European Broadcasting Union (EBU). Eurikon, their first project, was an experiment carried out on a broadcaster-to-broadcaster basis for five non-consecutive weeks in 1982 (Clarke 1983, p.29). Five EBU members – the IBA (UK), RAI (Italy), ORF (Austria), NOS (Netherlands) and ARD (then West Germany) – transmitting to 15 countries in turn for a week, tested the pan-European appeal of their programmes and tried to identify a 'pan-national editorial viewpoint' for their news services (Clarke 1984, p.50). Following the limited success of the experiment, and lengthy negotiations at the EBU, the RTE from Ireland and RTP from Portugal joined three of the Eurikon participants (NOS, ARD and RAI) to launch Europa on 5 October 1985.

Europa (based at the NOS studios in Hilversum), started with a handicap since most of the heavyweight EBU members refused to get involved. The French Antenne 2 and FR3 and the German ZDF feared that it would jeopardise their own TV5 and SAT3. Likewise, the BBC stayed away because it was not convinced with the quality of the project and had plans of its own (Papathanassopoulos 1990, p.60). To make matters worse, Europa was moulded in the public broadcasting ethos of its backers, it did not pay enough attention to audience tastes and broadcast too many highbrow programmes. The running costs were high (vast sums were spent on translation), the channel reached too few homes and failed to attract any significant advertising revenue. The Dutch broadcaster, which was unwilling to carry on assuming much of the financial costs, put its colleagues out of their misery and switched off the signal on 27 November 1986, 13 months after the launch (O'Connor 1986, p.54; Collins 1998, pp.143-9).

Europa had specific difficulties but the debacle was symptomatic of a difficult period for satellite television. At the root of the problem was the size of the reception universe that international TV channels tried to reach. Only 18 million European households were connected to cable until 1989, too small a figure to build a viable audience for advertisers (Woodman 1999, p.32). During the 1980s, the record distribution was reached by Sky Channel, with 15 million connections, closely followed by Super Channel (13.5 million homes), but the other channels never broke the 5 million mark (Snow 1987, p.22; Matthias 1987, p.27; Tallantire, 1989).

Another difficulty for cross-border channels was gaining access to foreign markets. Since the implementation of the Television Without Frontiers directive in 1991, channels can broadcast throughout Europe holding a single licence, because European Union member states are no longer allowed to stop international TV transmissions from other member states. Before this ground-breaking piece of legislation, international TV channels needed to go through a lengthy process of authorisation with local authorities. Government officials rarely knew how to deal with these requests and passed them on from one ministry to another. Once the appropriate department had been pinned down and assuaged, the consent of the local PTT was also needed to downlink the signal (Matthias 1987, p.27). The next task was to find cable operators and secure access on their networks. The cable industry was very fragmented and several partners were necessary to cover the main areas of a territory. Furthermore, the capacity of analogue networks was limited and cable providers were in the position of cherry-picking channels they wished to carry. Foreign-language channels were often dropped because they were seen as least relevant to their audience (Ritchie 1994, p.18).

The problems of cross-border TV channels were compounded by the dearth of the pan-European advertising market. Satellite television lacked a sizeable – and measurable – audience that would have tempted advertisers to transfer some of their budget to transnational television. The small number of multinationals that might have been interested in running international campaigns usually devolved marketing to their local affiliates which passed on the advertising budget to a local agency (Syfret 1989, p.55). Thus the pool of advertisers was limited to a few brands that were sold uniformly across the continent and could benefit from a regional advertising campaign.

By the early 1990s, the pan-European TV industry looked doomed. Cross-border channels lacked an audience, did not attract near enough advertising revenue and struggled to put together a coherent schedule. The most hyped transnational channel of the time, MTV, was assailed by emerging local competitors such as France's MCM, Germany's VIVA and Italy's Videomusic (Clover 1993). Industry analysts agreed that transnational satellite television had little prospect on the continent. They were openly sceptical when a group of EBU members launched Euronews on 1 January 1993 and they continued to predict the death of transnational television as late as 1998 (e.g. Barker 1993, p.32; Alonzi 1998).

The coming of age of satellite television in Europe

By the mid-1990s, the pan-European TV industry had matured and consolidated. Newcomers who had tried to enter the television industry via the pan-European route had left the market. The well-established broadcasters who had underestimated the difficulties of international television had either retreated to their home markets or learnt from their mistakes and re-designed their channels. The players who survived the early years acquired expertise in transnational broadcasting and were more confident about the future. These included CNN, which had arrived in Europe in September 1985, and MTV, which followed suit two years later. Sky News, one of the four British channels Murdoch launched in 1988, was made freely available in Europe the same year. In 1989, News International launched Eurosport in partnership with 16 members of the EBU as the American documentary network, Discovery, crossed the Atlantic.

Public service broadcasters continued to launch international channels, adding to TV5 and SAT3. Arte, a high-brow cultural channel, went on air in 1991 following a Franco-German treaty. Two years later, Euronews was started by 11 members of the EBU in answer to CNN's dominance of international news during the first Gulf War. In 1995, the BBC replaced BBC TV Europe (launched in June 1987) with BBC Prime, a subscription-based entertainment channel, and BBC World, a news channel supported by advertising.

The 1990s were also characterized by the arrival of American commercial broadcasters. Cartoon Network, operated by Turner Broadcasting System (an AOL Time Warner subsidiary), arrived in

Europe in 1994. Two years later, CNBC (Dow Jones and NBC) and Bloomberg started two European financial and business news channels. Fox Kids, controlled by Disney since 2001, and VH1 (Viacom's second music television network with MTV) also began in 1996. National Geographic started in 1997, and the following year Universal Television Network introduced Studio Universal and 13th Street in the largest markets in Europe.

These channels have had considerably more success than their predecessors. After years of deficit, most of them are showing reasonable returns on investment. The key factor was that the number of households connected to cable and satellite finally got large enough to provide a viable market for cross-border TV channels. In 2001, the number of households connected to cable and satellite reached 75.7 million homes in the European Union, representing 51.7 per cent of all TV households (European Audiovisual Observatory 2002, pp.38-9). The collapse of communist regimes in Central and Eastern Europe in the late 1980s brought an additional 31.3 million connected households by 2001 (ibid.). The total 2001 figure of 107 million homes represents a fourfold increase compared to the 1991 figure of 25.1 million cabled homes (Woodman 1999, p.32).

Cross-border TV channels have also benefited from the development of a new technology in the 1990s: direct-to-home (DTH) satellite broadcasting. The Astra 1A, launched in December 1988, was the first satellite powerful enough to allow reception with small dishes and low-cost equipment. DTH has opened whole new markets for satellite channels in countries that were poorly cabled, notably in Southern and Central/Eastern Europe. It has also given access to many more channels to viewers in cabled areas, adding the choice of satellite platforms to existing cable networks. DTH has grown exponentially since 1988 to become European's preferred reception mode. Among the 107 million connected households, 75.7 million (71 per cent) receive satellite channels directly at home (European Audiovisual Observatory 2002, pp.38-9).

The distribution of satellite channels further accelerated with the digitisation of cable and satellite networks in the late 1990s. Signal compression freed up much needed space on these networks, which were able to offer a far greater variety of channels to subscribers. As a result, cable and satellite operators no longer squeezed transnational channels out of their platforms. An added advantage of signal compression is that many more channels can fit into the transponders of communications satellites, lowering the cost of international transmission by a factor of six.

The current size of the reception universe is significant for two reasons. It has enabled the leading cross-border TV channels to develop their reach across Europe. Over recent years, their distribution has grown from an average of 33.3 million to 47.8 million TV households, and the two leading pan-European channels, Eurosport and MTV, currently stand just below the threshold of 100 million households (see Table 1).

Table 1: Full-time distribution of the leading 16 pan-European television channels, 1997-2002 (in million of TV households)

	1997	1998	1999	2000	2001	2002
Arte	/	78.9	61.9	61.9	65.0	65.0
BBC Prime	/	/	/	8.2	10.5	10.8
BBC World	25.1	33.1	39.3	45.5	49.4	56.4
Bloomberg	/	27.7	10.3	24.6	30.1	37.6
Cartoon Network	/	/	/	21.0	28.6	26.9
CNBC Europe	12.6	21.0	26.7	32.9	40.2	41.9
CNN International	58.9	67.8	68.8	73.2	81.0	84.7
Discovery	7.0	16.3	20.4	26.7	31.4	32.9
Eurosport	71.9	75.6	80.6	88.3	93.0	95.3
Euronews	30.4	34.3	34.9	34.0	44.0	48.9
Fox Kids	/	/	15.4	23.1	25.0	31.0
MTV	44.0	58.8	79.1	83.6	94.2	92.8
National Geographic	4.0	14.9	15.3	19.2	22.9	26.9
Sky News	/	/	38.9	18.6	22.7	24.0
TV5	45.5	55.7	57.6	66.1	68.0	71.4
VH1	/	/	20.3	23.1	19.1	18.5
Average distribution	33.3	44	40.7	39.1	45.3	47.8

Sources: *Media and Marketing Europe Guide: Pan-European Television*, 1998 to 2002

In addition, the reception universe is now large enough to sustain the development of smaller transnational channels that specialise in sub-genres, such as those that concentrate on a specific music style or type of documentary. Channels with a focused proposition and a narrow subscription base in terms of demographics need a European-wide distribution to leverage costs over more than one market and create economies of scale. This applies to all cross-border channels but particularly to the newer 'super-niche' channels such as E!Entertainment (celebrity news and entertainment) and Reality TV.

Financial health was also brought by the growth in advertising revenues. Between 1988 and 2001, the value of the pan-European advertising market has increased from 31 million Euros to 628 million Euros (Collins 1992, p.44; *Media and Marketing Europe Guide: Pan-European Television* 2002, p.16). The number of advertisers on pan-European TV grew from an estimated 200 in the late 1980s to more than 600 in 2002 (Syfret 1987, p.34). There has been a surge of products and services sold on a multinational basis. For instance, banks, such as UBS and HSBC, and insurance companies (e.g. AXA and Allianz), frequently advertise on international television, reflecting the trans-border scope of their activities.

Thus, several factors have combined to sustain the development of transnational television in the course of the 1990s. The expansion of the reception universe has enabled cross-border channels to increase coverage and leverage costs over many more markets, direct-to-home broadcasting has facilitated reception, digitisation has increased network capacity and viewers' choice, the growth of supply on communications satellites has lowered transmission costs, and the money spent on international advertising has increased twenty-fold in less than 15 years.

Struggling for local relevance

The successful expansion of cross-border channels stands in contrast to the amount of influence they hold in European culture and politics. The gap can be highlighted by comparing Europe with the Middle East. There, most satellite television channels lose money but have a wide audience and carry great clout in regional politics. The independent voice of Al-Jazeera has unsettled governments and forced them to take action, including launching their own satellite stations. Trans-border channels have introduced the most innovative TV formats and driven changes in Arab television. For instance, MBC (now Al-Arabiya) has raised the standard of broadcasting journalism and news reporting in the region (Sakr 2001; El-Nawawy, M. and A. Iskandar 2002). In Europe, international news TV channels have the privilege of being watched by the corporate and political elite yet their audience share is so small that they do not always show up in audience surveys. European transnational TV channels might be affluent but struggle for recognition beyond their niche audience.

The first reason toward explaining this contrast is that Europe is not as culturally and linguistically homogeneous as the Middle East. There, satellite channels are popular because, amongst other reasons, the region's residents share a language and an interest in many social, cultural and political issues. Europe remains a mosaic of cultures, languages and lifestyles, and it is exceedingly difficult to build a transnational audience in such an environment.

Secondly, the European broadcasting market is more mature than the Middle East and thus competition is fierce. In the 1990s, although the number of cable and satellite homes in Europe was growing, a fast increasing number of national channels were competing for the same audience. Between 1991 and 2000, the number of cable and satellite channels grew from 145 to 1013, thus saturating niche markets such as children's, movies and sport (*Screen Digest*, March 2001, p.87). National news and music television channels began eating into the audience share of CNN and MTV. The distribution of pan-European TV channels was progressing but ratings remained stagnant. It dawned on international broadcasters that the region was too competitive a market for television services that might be seen as foreign and irrelevant to viewers. To carry on in business, cross-border channels had to address the issue of local relevance and begin by adapting to local tastes. This has led to the emergence of practices of localisation and to the mutation of international feeds into local channels.

There exist different ways of localising a cross-border signal. The most basic technique is to introduce a local language, which can be achieved through translation or multi-lingual service. Translation involves either dubbing or subtitling, depending on the broadcaster's resources and the audience. Territories where English is a strong second language, such as Scandinavia or the Netherlands, get more subtitles than do the French or Portuguese. Discovery subtitles its documentaries in 22 languages whilst Cartoon Network dubs its cartoons in 9 languages. Multi-lingual service consists of covering the same video track with different commentaries and is predominantly employed for live programming. Both Euronews and Eurosport cover their main feed with 7 and 18 languages respectively. The francophone TV5 has introduced sub-titles in seven languages, including Dutch and Portuguese, to help French learners. Using one method or another, the leading 16 pan-European TV channels broadcast on average in eight languages. BBC World, Sky News and VH1 are the only channels to broadcast solely in English (*Media and Marketing Europe Guide: Pan-European Television*, 2002, pp. 22-3).

Transnational TV channels can also split their video signal and introduce local programming windows for specific territories lasting from a few minutes to several hours. National Geographic has introduced devolved programming in eight European countries and CNN International broadcast three 15-minute news bulletins in Germany.

Localisation procedures might help cross-border channels remain relevant in a multicultural environment, but cannot on their own iron out all difficulties associated with transnational television. Cross-border feeds are notoriously complex to schedule because of the different lifestyles and viewing habits across Europe. For instance, the peak viewing in Scandinavia time is earlier (7pm) than in France (8pm) or Spain (10pm). Holidays and school days vary from country to country, presenting children's channels with an acute problem. Multi-lingual tracks address the language issue but prevent commentaries from being read on-camera by a presenter. Euronews and Eurosport's main feeds are faceless and therefore have experienced difficulty in building an identity. Tastes and interests vastly differ throughout Europe. Eurosport's retransmissions of, for example, ski jumping and Nordic skiing competitions are of little interest to Southern European audiences. Football might be popular across Europe, but team following remains domestic. As MTV found out in the early 1990s, Europeans' tastes in music are far too eclectic to be covered by a single feed.

In addition, different market conditions prevail in each country, as determined by broadcasting legislation and policy, the shape of the distribution platforms and the weight of public service broadcasting. For instance, the French government has reinforced the quota requirements outlined by the European directive Television Without Frontiers, requesting that television schedules contain at least 60 per cent of programming of European origin. Local regulatory regimes regarding decency, swearing and nudity remain very different across Europe, requiring channels to be cautious about some of the material they broadcast. All these factors have brought international broadcasters to conclude that their expansion goals will only be met by a responsive approach to local realities.

Since the mid-1990s, many broadcasters have begun shifting to the practice of international networking, which can be defined as the creation of a network of local channels around a core broadcasting philosophy. The local channels share a concept, brand, part of the programming and library titles, resources and infrastructures, and teamwork, but develop according to their respective environment. They employ local staff, register with local regulatory bodies, and set up their own schedule mixing shared network content with their own material. Local teams have the advantage of being able to exchange ideas, knowledge and experience with other teams. Whilst they benefit from the network's global expertise, the network takes advantage of their local knowledge.

The existing networks in Europe cover the continent with an average of 8.5 channels, using a mix of country- and region-specific channels (see Table 2). Some broadcasters privilege region-specific feeds, like Discovery, whilst Bloomberg concentrates its efforts on country-specific operations.

Table 2: Pan-European television networks

	Country-specific channels	Region-specific channels
Bloomberg	France, Italy, Spain, UK	Germany +1
Cartoon Network	France, Spain, Italy, the Netherlands, Poland	Central & Eastern Europe, Scandinavia, UK +2
Discovery	Denmark, Italy, Poland	Benelux, Central Europe, Eastern Europe, Germany +, Scandinavia, Spain & Portugal, UK +
Fox Kids	France, Greece, Italy, the Netherlands, Poland, Spain	Central & Eastern Europe, Germany +, Hungary and Czech Republic, Scandinavia, UK +
MTV	France, Italy, the Netherlands, Poland, Romania, Spain	Germany +, Scandinavia, UK +
Turner Classic Movies	France, Spain, Italy, the Netherlands, Poland	Central & Eastern Europe, Scandinavia, UK +

Sources: interviews and company literature
1 Includes Austria and German-speaking Switzerland.
2 Includes Ireland.

MTV, Cartoon Network, Discovery and Turner Classic Movies have progressively regionalised their pan-European feeds, whilst Bloomberg and Fox Kids have started with local channels and gradually increased their reach across Europe. Some of these networks run pan-European feeds in parallel to their local channels, either as a complement to existing channels (Bloomberg) or to fill the gaps (sometimes momentarily) between their country/region-specific channels (Cartoon Network and MTV). Cartoon Network broadcast slightly localised versions of its pan-European feed in Central Europe to test whether the markets can sustain a local channel. It launched its first country-specific channel in the UK in 1994, quickly followed by MTV in Italy. Bloomberg started its European operations in France in 1995, and Fox Kids launched in Britain the following year.

Europe's most extensive network is that of MTV, with five country-specific and four region-specific channels spanning the continent. Soon after MTV had launched a devolved service in Italy, it split its pan-European feed into MTV North, covering most of Europe, and MTV Central, servicing the German-speaking countries. In 1997, MTV UK & Ireland and MTV Nordic were launched. A second wave of local channels appeared in Poland, the Netherlands, Spain and France in 2000, and most recently in Romania. MTV has made considerable investments in its network, opening large production centres in places like Milan and Munich, each employing around 150 staff.

Networks constitute the most elaborate answer to the difficulties of operating TV channels across frontiers, allowing broadcasters to combine global leverage with local adaptability. Within a network, channels always share some attributes but can differentiate themselves as much as required by market conditions. They can develop their own schedule, acquire and produce material locally and modify the brand positioning according to the local audience and competition. As a result, subscribers of the same pan-European TV network end up watching quite different channels.

Addressing a multinational audience

The pan-European television industry has prospered by adapting to the region's cultural diversity and juggling between two dimensions, the local and the global. Many transnational channels have transformed into networks of local channels that may share some programming but adopt local mores. Only a few channels remain that address an international public and do not follow the strategy of dividing a multinational market into distinct audiences. They have kept a commitment to the transnational and have succeeded in making the international an integral part of their brand and programming.

Both BBC World and CNN broadcast a single feed in Europe and have designed a range of programmes tailored to a multinational audience. In addition to the international news bulletins broadcast on the hour, the BBC World's news programmes include *World Business Today* and *Sport Today*. The channel has also developed a range of factual programmes that are international in scope. These include *Reporters* (reflective international journalism), *Correspondent* (observational reporting from the BBC's correspondents across the globe), *Simpson's World* (analysis from the corporation's world affairs editor John Simpson), *Earth Report* (environment) and *Extra Time* (sport).

In October 1987, CNN launched the first global newscast, the *World Report*, which includes unedited news reports from a multitude of broadcasters. Today, the network transmits a number of programmes that bring international news to its audience, such as *World News* (scheduled throughout the day), *World Sport*, *World Business*, *Business International* and *International Correspondents*. The London bureau also produces two shows with a European focus: *World News Europe*, which provides a daily news update from a European perspective, and *Inside Europe*, a more analytical programme on Europe's topical issues.

Euronews has a commitment to Europe. Whilst the channel is independent from European political institutions, European matters lie at the heart of the channel's news agenda. Many of the channel's programmes are European in scope, including *Europa* and *Parlamento*, on the European Union and the European Parliament, and current affairs magazines *Europeans*, focusing on topical issues, and *Perspectives*, which brings a European angle to the world's leading stories.

CNBC, the financial and business news channel, has kept a pan-regional feed to cover Europe that is adapted to the re-structuring of the financial sector in the region over the past decade. In addition to the European currency, bringing twelve currencies together and creating a European Central Bank, two leading derivatives exchanges have formed: London-based Euronext.liffe and the German-Swiss rival, Eurex, which regroups four stock exchanges (Amsterdam, Brussels, Paris and Lisbon). Banks and brokerage firms have re-organised their operations and no longer approach the market country-by-country but on a sector-by-sector basis that spans Europe. European CEOs like to give interviews to CNBC because the majority of their corporate shareholders live outside the country.

Arte's mission is to become one of Europe's leading cultural channels. It was created on the basis of the Franco-German treaty of 2

October 1990, and the agreements of cooperation signed by the channel with several public broadcasters over the past five years are helping it expand its remit. It has not yet reached a pan-regional distribution but its European dimension is further emphasized by the current relocation of its headquarters to Strasbourg.

These channels reach a European public, albeit on a limited scale. The audience they address is largely composed of the political and business elite who need to be kept informed of regional and global developments for professional reasons. Evidence shows that, within this group, a majority watch transnational TV and appreciate watching stations that rise above the parochial angle characterizing national broadcasters' news coverage. The pan-European TV industry commission an annual audience survey conducted by Ipsos in 16 European countries. The survey universe is restricted to individuals with a personal annual income of at least 45,000 Euros and who either travel at least six times a year or hold the post of company director. The resulting sample's average respondent has an annual income of 80,000 Euros and holds investments worth 352,000 Euros. 20 per cent of these own three cars or more and 12 per cent possess their own art collection. 74 per cent of the respondents watch a pan-European TV channel at least once a month, 61 per cent at least once a week and 29 per cent every day. On a weekly basis, CNN International is the most frequently watched news channel, followed by Euronews, BBC World and CNBC. This translates into 3.1 million viewers per week for CNN, 2.0 million for Euronews, 1.6 million for BBC World and 1 million viewers for CNBC (Ipsos-IRL 2003).

Conclusion: Towards a European Public Sphere?

These channels might reach a European-wide public, but do they constitute an embryonic European public sphere? Are they the watchdog that holds European institutions accountable for their decisions? Do they help form a European common awareness? Do they foster pan-regional debates on European issues? Stig Hjarvard raised such questions ten years ago and the answer must remain negative (1993). Today, one can be even more pessimistic since the recent expansion of transnational TV networks has had little impact on the formation of a regional public sphere. Even the broadcasters that have kept a pan-regional feed are aware of the limits of this market and try to expand with local channels. CNN has a series of joint ventures with partners in Spain (CNN +), Germany (N-TV) and Turkey (CNN Türk), and CNBC operates channels in Italy (CFN-CNBC) and Turkey (CNBC-E). As for Euronews, in March 2003 France Television bought 49 per cent of the consortium's shares held by the London-based news production company ITN since 1997. Adding to the 20 per cent shares France Television already held, this move leaves the door open for a transformation of Euronews into a CNN *à la française* – a long-held dream of many members of the French governmental Gaullist majority.

The emergent pan-European public does not extend much beyond a transnational managerial class. Audience surveys show that whilst international channels are relatively popular within this group, they rarely pass the one per cent mark of audience share (European Audiovisual Observatory 2002). There is no channel with a large European audience. Very little news or factual programming has a regional following and no talkshow inflames opinions across Europe. The activities and decisions of European institutions are still largely publicised by the national media. If a regional public sphere is developing, it excludes the bulk of European citizenry.

Europe is the world's most advanced transnational democracy. As James Anderson writes, the European Union is a 'pioneering association of national states with innovative 'multi-level' and 'cross-border' forms of governance and a 'sharing' of sovereignty' (2002, p. 3). But the evolution of European television has not matched the pioneering developments of cross-border governance. European cultural diversity has kept Europe a fragmented TV market. Despite the European Commission's attempt to create a single audiovisual market, no pan-European media space has yet emerged. More than twenty years after the first satellite TV channel in Europe, there is no regional public sphere that coexists alongside regional institutions such as the European Parliament and the European currency. Does this situation reflect the nature of European integration as an elite-driven project in which the European citizenry has had little involvement? At the very least, doubts can be raised about the participatory nature of a trans-border democracy that lacks the media spaces to sustain direct participation of large sections of the European public.

References

Alonzi, T. 1998, 'Growing up is hard to do', *Media and Marketing Europe Guide: Pan-European Television*, pp. 18-19.

Anderson, J. 2002, 'Introduction', in *Transnational Democracy: Political Spaces and Border Crossings*, ed. James Anderson, Routledge, London, pp. 1-5.

Barker, P. 1993 'Nouvelles cuisine', *Cable and Satellite Europe*, February, p. 32-4.

Barrand, C. 1986, 'Europa Television – The Transponder's Eye View', *EBU Review. Programmes, Administration, Law*, vol. 37, no. 2, pp. 10-13.

Clarke, N. 1982, 'Pan-European TV?', *Irish Broadcasting Review*, vol. 14, Summer, pp. 42-7.

Clarke, N. 1983, 'Eurikon promises a new programme concept', *Intermedia*, vol. 11, no. 3, pp. 29-30.

Clarke, N. 1984, 'The Birth of the Infant Eurikon', *Intermedia*, vol. 12, no. 2, pp. 50-1.

Julian Clover, J. 1993, 'Playing it by ear', *Cable and Satellite Europe,* February, pp. 18-24.

Collins, R. 1992, *Satellite Television in Western Europe – Revised edition*, John Libbey, London.

Collins, R. 1998, *From Satellite to Single Market: New Communication Technology and European Public Service Television*, Routledge, London.

European Audiovisual Observatory 2002, *Yearbook Volume 1: Economy of the European Audiovisual Industry*, European Audiovisual Observatory, Strasbourg.

El-Nawawy, M. and A. Iskandar 2002, *Al-Jazeera: How the Free Arab News Network Scooped the World and Changed the Middle East*, Westview Press, Cambridge, MA.

Fry, A. 2002, 'Minority Pursuit', *Cable and Satellite Europe*, January/February, pp. 20-6.

Hjarvard, S. 1993, 'Pan-European Television News: Towards A European Political Public Sphere?', in *National Identity and Europe: The Television Revolution*, eds P. Drummond, R. Paterson and J. Willis, BFI, London, pp. 71-94.

Ipsos-IRL 2003, *Europe 2003: A Survey of Decision Makers and Leading Consumers*, Ipsos-IRL, Harrow.

Matthias, G. 1987, 'Many happy connections', *Cable and Satellite Europe,* November, pp. 27-30.

O'Connor, V. 1986, 'Climbing a Euro-mountain', *Cable and Satellite Europe*, July, p. 54-5.

Papathanassopoulos, S. 1990, 'Towards European Television: The Case of Europa-TV', *Media Information Australia*, vol. 56, May, pp. 57-63.

Ritchie, C. 1994, 'Crunch time for cable', *Cable and Satellite Europe*, May, pp. 18-20.

Sakr, N. 2001, *Satellite Realms: Transnational Television, Globalization and the Middle East*, I.B. Tauris, London.

Snow, N. 1987, 'Europa: End of a dream', *Cable and Satellite Europe*, January, p. 22.

Syfret, T. 1989, 'A Recall for the Euro-ad?', *Cable and Satellite Europe*, April, pp. 55-7.

Syfret, T. 1987, 'Commercial breaks', *Cable and Satellite Europe*, January, pp. 33-4.

Tallantire, M. 1989, 'Falling from Sky', *Cable and Satellite Europe*, July, pp. 29-31.

Tallantire, M. 1994, 'The Beginnings of Empire', *Cable and Satellite Europe*, January, pp. 32-4.

Woodman, C. 1999, '15 years of intelligence', *Cable and Satellite Europe*, May, pp. 30-4.

A Structural Bias against Pan-European TV?
Stewart Purvis

In 1997 the British commercial news provider ITN bought an operating stake in the pan-European news channel, *EuroNews*. The deal caused a flurry of interest in some sections of the Europe-wide media.

The Economist believed that ITN was taking on quite a task by trying to operate a company in a public-private partnership with shareholders from 20 different European public broadcasters. 'Good luck, ITN' they concluded sceptically. One week later *The European* newspaper covered the news of the ITN deal. Their conclusion 'Good luck, ITN' again.

Five and a half years later *The European* doesn't exist anymore (I am tempted to say 'Bad Luck, *The European*') but *EuroNews* still does and has developed to become the most-watched news channel in Europe. But ITN has ended its connection with the channel. Instead *EuroNews* is back as a public channel in negotiation for various forms of public funding.

Why and how that happened is a significant indicator of key structural issues in the European media. As the Chief Executive of ITN for 8 years until my retirement this summer, I have long argued that public broadcasters, and particularly publicly funded broadcasters, need to be more analytical in arguing for their special rights and privileges. 'If we didn't exist, nobody else would do it' has become a lazy *raison d'être* for too many broadcasters. As commercially funded broadcasters provide an increasing number of high quality services, alongside the many low quality programmes they also transmit, public broadcasters need to do better than just parrot the traditional mantra of self-justification.

Arguing this cause has often seen me labelled as a 'critic' of the BBC; in fact I believe the BBC is more likely to survive if it confronts this issue, as it increasingly has had to do. So against this background, it may surprise some that five years in the pan-European television business has led me to the conclusion that publicly-funded intervention in this crowded market is justified because the market is structurally biased against a service like *EuroNews* which attempts to be truly pan-European.

The contrast between the on-screen success of *EuroNews* and its commercial disappointment is striking. In Europe 3.9 million viewers watch *EuroNews* daily either on cable or satellite - twice as many as CNN and three times bigger than BBC World. Its higher audience figures are partly explained by the fact that it transmits in many of the different languages of Europe, not just English but also French, German, Spanish, Italian, Portuguese, Russian and - for part of the day - Danish. Whatever the spread of English as the de facto language of Europe, people like to watch TV in their own language. Another 2.1 million see some of the channel's programmes re-broadcast on the partners' channels such as FR3 in France. The total number of homes where the channel can be seen at some time in the day is now 137 million.

EuroNews was the first news channel to transmit in Russian to the people of Russia on their own air-waves. A partnership with the Russian broadcaster *RTR* has taken it onto a terrestrial network in Moscow, as well as cable and satellite. And on the opposite side of the globe my other proud moment as President of the Channel was overseeing a deal which took *EuroNews* onto the main New York cable system, *Cablevision*.

So how come against this background, ITN only managed to get the channel into profit once in five years, and that partly helped by the licence fees which the partner broadcasters pay for the right to transmit parts of the channel on their own airwaves?

There are four explanations. First and foremost is the structure of European advertising markets where commercial airtime sales teams remain resolutely nationally based, despite the take-overs which have brought the practitioners into Europe-wide companies and the growth of the cross-border brands which they promote in many European countries.

Whoever owns what and sells what, the people who decide where television advertisements are placed prefer to put them on the channels that they and their clients are most familiar with. And because the spending decisions are made by clients who are nationally based, their agents - the airtime sales buyers - think national, not pan-European. The growth of cable and satellite has offered them yet more national media to advertise on.

As a result the channels which launched in the belief that this was a practice which would change as Europe changed have been disappointed. Many, including one of the first, *Superchannel*, have come and gone. The exceptions are *Eurosport*, because the appeal of sport cross-borders has created ratings which advertisers can't ignore, and *CNN*, whose brand, if not its ratings, crosses borders well. But for a range of mostly factually based channels the size of the revenue market has barely grown and holding their share of that market has got tougher.

The second reason for the problems of such channels is that nationally based news broadcasters are themselves in the cross-border business, if only because the topography of Europe means transmitters take no account of national frontiers, and nor do satellites. So the factual TV market is sliced again.

And that's before you add in the American-owned channels for whom Europe is a brand extension helping to get themselves better known globally as much as a proper business opportunity.

And the final dose of cold water on pan-European news as a business is that languages cost money.

The *EuroNews* newsroom in Lyons with its seven different language teams and countless more nationalities within those language groups is unique. It is a stimulating and inspiring place to be on a big news day, with journalists working together to make the seven different language tracks not just to fit the common video feed but to inform and explain the events of the day. But it costs seven times what an equivalent national single-language newsroom would cost.

So having got *EuroNews* into profit at least one year but only one, ITN decided that, although history was on our side and that eventually cross-border advertising sales might one day become the norm and match the costs of multi-lingualism, we couldn't afford to wait for history. The torch of funding a truly-Europe wide approach to news is now carried by those 20 different European public broadcasters (its 19 actually) and by the European institutions which have, I believe, a proper right to fund where market failure occurs, and a healthy vested interest in helping Europeans (and non-Europeans around the world) know more about Europe.

Media Coverage of the European Union
Professor David Morgan

The UK has been a member of the European Community/Union (EU) since 1972. A partner in Europe yes – but from early days an 'Awkward Partner' as Stephen George put it in his book in 1990. Though the 1975 referendum result which confirmed British membership was overwhelming, a large section of the Labour Party and some Conservatives voted against. The arrival of Mrs. Thatcher as Prime Minister in 1979 initiated years of tension over Europe and, eventually, a change of heart within the Labour Party. Despite her rhetoric, Mrs. Thatcher signed treaties which increased European integration and left her successor, John Major, with the task of leading a Conservative Party divided on the issue of Europe. With the advent of a Labour government under Tony Blair in May 1997 the outlook seemed set fair for further European integration including re-entry into the European Monetary Union (EMU) if a referendum approved this.

Since the 1975 referendum British public opinion has been generally supportive of EU membership, but with reservations. After 1980 support began to weaken, so that by the 2001 Election most Conservative MPs, and a growing minority of Labour MPs, were Eurosceptics. In the 170 marginal seats the Conservatives needed to win to oust Labour, 78 of their candidates were opposed to EMU entry, 81 accepted the 'not in the next parliament' position, while only 11 were pro EMU. Popular opinion remains divided over EMU with a clear majority against. The Labour government is agnostic on the question until the Treasury's 'Five Economic Tests' for entry are passed and confirmed in a referendum. The UK continues to be the 'Awkward Partner' in the EU.

This phenomenon needs to be seen in context, and that context has two parts: first the party political context and second the European media context.

The Political Context of European Coverage

Membership of the EU has been central to British politics and the British economy since the 1980s and large bodies of opinion in government, the professions and trade unions doubt whether there can be significant change in this. Stability in Europe is vital to British security and the EU is Britain's biggest market. Only by being full and enthusiastic members can both be assured. Pro-EU groups combine those who are pro by conviction and those who see no alternative.

Groups which are labelled Eurosceptic, however, combine those opposed to any European 'state' on a variety of grounds and those who think they see alternatives. For these the EU suffers from serious economic and political deficiencies. For some Eurosceptics, the EU is a nascent European super-state characterised by Franco-German dominance, the transfer of resources from northern to southern Europe and, prospectively, to eastern Europe. For others, the EU is a dated, failing attempt to build a peaceful and prosperous Europe able to resist US or Japanese economic hegemony.

Underpinning both propositions are two deeply held convictions: firstly, the notion that the nation state is the irreducible actor in the international system, and secondly, that the EU is anachronistic now that the Cold War has ended. What made sense at a continental level two generations ago is a nonsense now in an increasingly globalised economy. On both counts, it is argued, EU fails because it is a project of European elites which after fifty years still suffers a visible democratic deficit which, rhetoric apart, is actually intensifying as those elites become fearful of failure.

Some British voters fear the loss of national independence. More are disturbed by what they see as the undemocratic nature of the EU's governing institutions. The elected European Parliament, they say, is no real check on the powerful European Commission – and the Council of Ministers with increasing use of Qualified Majority Voting is not a satisfactory mechanism for protecting British interests. Some British concerns may be rooted in generalised historical xenophobia and ignorance of the EU which the events of the 20th Century have reinforced. Major wars resulting in loss of empire and diminished relative influence are, unsurprisingly, not likely to endear the EU in the eyes of British voters, even if those same wars helped strengthen pan-European sentiment in most continental states.

Not often mentioned but undoubtedly present in British government thinking is the attitude of the US government to the EU. Initially supportive, the US administration is disturbed by anti-American attitudes visible in trade negotiations, and even more disturbed when France and Germany talk of a European defence identity which excludes the US. The British economy, for many Eurosceptics, is more compatible with the American economy, and UK governments have been concerned over anti-NATO sentiments voiced, particularly in France. British trading patterns, and trading ambitions, are more globally oriented than those of most EU members. The UK is not seen by many Conservatives as 'European' in its history and culture, and for them its future security and trading interests are better served by closer Atlantic links.

These debates are at least thirty years old and have been the cause of bitter divisions within and between parties. Until the mid 70s the British Left continued to see the European Community as a capitalist structure which should be resisted. Not until the mid 1980s was a new generation of Labour leaders able to reverse this and present a European Union as a vehicle for social democracy. The Conservative party under Edward Heath was enthusiastically pro-European. Under Mrs. Thatcher it strove to limit European integration except on matters affecting free trade, since many Conservatives had come to see the European Union as potentially a socialist Trojan horse. Mrs. Thatcher's successor, John Major, found the greatest difficulty in holding his cabinet and party together on Europe, especially after withdrawal from EMU in 1993, and was swept out of power by New Labour in 1997.

The New Labour government professed to have a large reformist agenda. This included electoral reform for national elections as well as proportional representation for European Parliament elections. Both steps seemed more 'democratic' and promised to keep the Conservatives out of office for the foreseeable future. Looking forward, this prospect would more than offset the significant loss of Labour members in the European Parliament to be elected in 1999. New Labour set about ending the situation in which the European Parliament was a refuge for 'old Labour' in Wales, Scotland and parts of England. A reselection process was put in hand in 1997 and became a staple news item in the coverage of EU matters, to the delight of the Conservatives. They, meanwhile, began to go through their own struggles over Europe as the new leadership made Eurosceptic attitudes essential for success in constituency candidate selection.

All of this made good copy for journalists. Labour maintained the facade of unity over the EU with Chancellor Gordon Brown's setting of rigorous tests for British re-entry into EMU. Journalists noted how the Conservatives became steadily more Eurosceptic, declaring that there could be no re-entry into EMU 'for the next Parliament.' Some Conservatives moved to a position of virtually seeking withdrawal from the Union. Newspapers like *The Guardian*, *The Independent* and *The Daily Mirror* championed the EU cause though not without reservations. Against them were ranged the stridently Eurosceptic *Daily Telegraph* and *Daily Mail* and the more complex Euroscepticism of *The Times*. The results of the local elections in May 1999 and more specifically the European Parliament elections in June 1999 at least suggested that public opinion was increasingly against further European integration. As the electorate grew more disillusioned with the prospect of European integration, the governing elite found itself more isolated in pursuing pro-EU policies.

The European Media Context

There is no simple relationship between what media coverage offers voters and what voters believe and act on. The influence of mass media on public opinion is a complex process of interaction between public trust in information provided by the media and previous personal experience of voters. The partisanship of unlicensed media – newspapers and magazines – is to an extent offset by the political non-partisanship of licensed and regulated radio and television. Voters are offered a wide range of information on all aspects of personal and societal activities – including government and politics – and filter this through the preferences they acquire from their own experiences and those of family and friends. Having said that, however, it is clear that political leaderships, if trusted, can be very influential on matters involving political decisions large and small. Elite consensus can build a public consensus over time and elite dissensus can change voter consensus.

The UK press – like the main political parties – is divided over the EU and particularly over EMU membership and the promised referendum. The debate in Britain focuses on identity and sovereignty questions, complicated by party divisions on the subject and by foreign ownership of some of the key newspapers on the Eurosceptic side – Rupert Murdoch's *Times* and *Sun* and Conrad Black's *Telegraph*. Radio and television aim to be non-partisan though inevitably there are allegations of bias against both BBC and ITV in the public and private discourse of some politicians. Certainly, in the opinion of Brussels officials, the British press is the least starry-eyed about the EU project. The UK might have given birth to the *Financial Times* – 'the EU house journal,' as it was described by one official – but it also produces some of the most acerbic and hostile (but highly knowledgeable) journalists seen at Brussels press conferences.

Press reporters from other European countries were more likely to be 'true believers' in the European ideal but, seen by Brussels officials, appear to be becoming more like the British press corps. In part this official opinion is based on the noticeable change in the amount and focus of EU news being put out by the media. The 1990s saw a 50 per cent increase over the previous decade in EU news items carried by the media in many member countries. The press services of the EU institutions believe that, in part, this was due to the greatly extended information facilities provided by them. Commission, Council, and Parliament documents can be publicly accessed online. MEPs have their own web-sites, as have the political groups in the European Parliament. The legislature has rented satellite television time to put selected debates and committee hearings before a global audience. Some journalists, of course, will argue that sanitised documents and set-piece occasions are simply a means of 'rewriting history.' They will always want to know 'What was excluded, and why?' Nevertheless, EU institutions have become much more accessible to interested parties and to the general public, and they believe their efforts are eroding the capacities of member governments to doctor EU information for their own domestic advantage.

Greater accessibility has also helped to change the balance of newsworthiness in favour of the European Parliament. In the early 1990s there was a heavy concentration on trade and monetary policy, on foreign and defence policies, areas where Parliament's role is limited. Inevitably therefore journalists focused on the Commission and the Council with the Parliament taking a back seat. This changed as Parliament became the vehicle for a rising tide of popular concern over unemployment, social deprivation, environmental and consumer matters. Parliamentary coverage in the press tripled by 1996 with MEPs being given considerably more space than before, in particular through MEP letters, articles and interviews. All of which should cause no surprise. As with other news, the coverage of EU news is bound to vary over time and between countries. It peaks when the Union is in crisis (Maastricht Treaty, Single European Act, European Monetary Union), when there are elections to the Parliament (1994, 1999), when the President is dominant (Jacques Delors) or when the Commissioners are under fire (1998 onwards). In short, EU news peaks when editors consider it newsworthy by normal news standards.

What was new in the 1990s was that increasingly EU news was being written by journalists based in their home countries – and sourced outside the EU institutions. Increased volume was one thing – and was welcomed by EU officials – but the focus was increasingly critical on all EU institutions on questions of employment (GATT, EMU) foreign and security policy (Yugoslavia and Russia) and corruption (the sleaze factor). Not only was the coverage critical, but the stress was on the national consequences of these failings for member states. Member governments were putting such consequences at the centre of their press briefings and there was little or no 'good news' from Brussels to contradict such briefings.

Why was this? The reasons are complex and, Brussels officials could argue, were not primarily about EU responsibilities. Tensions arose between members of the EU and NATO over Yugoslavia, over GATT negotiations, over terms of trade with less developed countries. These issues mixed both economic and security competencies and the EU was resented when it tried to be pro-active e.g. by France over GATT and the UK over Yugoslavia.

If trade and security policy problems dominated the mid-1990s, journalists found themselves having to cover other divisive issues a little later. The impact of rapid economic change and rising unemployment – blamed by most on globalisation – weakened and then helped topple the conservative governments of Germany and the UK while constraining socialist coalitions all over the EU. The successor governments in the UK and Germany, though ostensibly social democratic, provided few panaceas and were quickly accused of failing their supporters. Allied to such problems were the increasing salience of questions such as immigration/asylum and the fears of a political backlash – exemplified in Austria, but present in all EU states. Governments were torn over abandoning the goals of the free movement of labour and the humanitarian treatment of needy groups and individuals. Journalistic copy recognised that governments had to limit the numbers of illegal immigrants while curbing the criminally run, exploitative 'traffic in human misery'. The fact that Western Europe needed more workers to support state pension schemes in face of ageing populations, and had skill shortages in many industries, was observed *sotto voce* in much media coverage. Questions of corruption at the European Commission and the 'gravy train' characteristics of the European Parliament provided journalists with seemingly conclusive evidence of graft and maladministration within the EU. Journalists could not fail to note that any eastward expansion of EU membership would only increase such doubts. It was, and remains, a news profile which in all member states both disturbs those in favour of further integration and thoroughly alarms the opponents of such a development.

Media Performance – the EU and the newsrooms.

How do journalists assess the quality of EU institutions as news sources? The following is based on interviews on both sides of the official – journalist line. How far was the news profile a product of this interface?

Of the EU institutions the European Parliament is seen by journalists as the most accessible and the European Council as the least. The Commission is seen as more or less accessible depending on the policy area and the Directorate General concerned. Areas of 'the high politics of integration,' as one journalist put it, are the least accessible while regional policy and the Common Agricultural Policy are much more so. Any area of policy, however, which threatens conflict tends to become less accessible as the Council approaches deadlock. Journalists looking at EU news see many constraints – national sensitivities, official favouritism towards national press corps, and official reluctance to have any publicity at all in some cases.

Sources are multiple, and not only in Brussels. Spokespersons for Commissioners, the office of the President, the national delegations in Brussels, MEPs, Party Groups and European Parliament officials, all provide useful information if it suits their purposes. Interest groups which proliferate in Brussels are good sources and can point to new sources in national governments and political circles in member states. The Directorates General are highly variable in their news provision and the quality of information officers varies considerably. Some are criticised for their lack of 'fit' with other sources in a Directorate General and their unjustified suspicion of British reporters generally. But overall so much information is offered that, as one British reporter put it, 'Here I sift, I don't have to dig.'

The overall incoherence visible in information strategies makes life difficult for all journalists and especially when officials blame them for reporting only what they have been told by other sources, including other officials. One journalist observed that the Commission is 'too full of true believers and they expect to address an audience of true believers.' Officials who are used to dealing with a largely party political continental press, and reporters from state radio and television networks, find British reporters often irreverent and sceptical of the information they provide. When such officials classify such reporters as hostile that only exacerbates problems with the coverage of the EU generally, as some officials are prepared to acknowledge.

Many of these problems are rooted in differing party, national and journalistic news cultures within member states. Some of the differences were exacerbated by Mrs. Thatcher's abrasive persona and adversarial political style in the 1980s. Many British journalists see real differences of attitude toward the EU among their colleagues in the International Press Centre in Brussels. These range from the more obedient Italian reporters through the frank chauvinism of the French to the more varied and sceptical German and Dutch media. For new British reporters it is hard at first to cope with the fragmented news-release style which is, as one broadsheet reporter put it, 'much more like Washington than London or Paris.'

Most British journalists have no orientation training before arrival and, to the surprise of some, find none on offer in Brussels. Used to learning 'on the job' and helped by colleagues from time to time, they have to learn the ropes quickly. Some freely admit that they are daunted by what one radio reporter called 'the multinational and multilingual aspects of the EU and their unparalleled detail.' For most of the 1990s the language of briefings was French and one senior reporter admitted that 'my schoolboy French is good enough for asking a question, but hopeless for grasping a complex answer.' Some reporters suspect that spokesmen deliberately exploited this weakness, but another, a fluent French speaker, denied this, saying, 'We are not about simple questions and answers here.' British reporters, and others too, have protested volubly about this, and English has now become a more usual language for media briefings than French – much to the annoyance of those more used to the previous dispensation.

Lack of orientation of some British reporters was made worse by changes in EU information policy. In the early and mid-1990s in the wake of the Maastricht Treaty the context was positive towards talk of greater integration, even to the point of federalism. This, said one reporter, meant that briefers favoured regional media in an effort to go around national press representatives. The monetary crisis and the first Danish referendum blunted this thrust and left reporters wondering what – if any – policy remained. The late 1990s saw something of a repeat of this cycle. 'Blairism' led to a renewal of efforts to 'sell' the EU in the UK but, since experience showed little change, there has been a regression to a situation described by one MEP as *festina lente.*'

Differences in EU information policy are paralleled by the alleged differing treatment of journalists by officials of different nationalities. French officials, as one British journalist put it, 'look to French journalists to get their message out' and this was a pattern not unknown among other officials and their fellow nationals in the press corps. But whatever the briefing patterns, there are differences also in the use made of information by the national press corps. As one British journalist noted, 'German journalists keep a low profile, the French are given to grand theorising, while the British are over-ready to build on little information.'

Journalists could thus be significant in playing up or playing down the information they lever out of the system. Into that process plays their own anticipation of how their stories will be seen back in their editorial offices. Editorial expectations were well understood, particularly when the 'facts' in Brussels allow a degree of calculated ambiguity about outcomes. Most British journalists have come to see that, since the early 1990s, the UK is no different from most other EU capitals which have all realised that EU had become, as one tabloid journalist observed, 'central to their interests.' Notwithstanding that, however, British journalists are only too aware that their audiences are likely to be more Eurosceptic than those in other countries. Journalists know that their stories from Brussels continue to be thought of as 'opaque and on the foreign page' except when their national political leaders choose to bring it forcibly to front page attention for domestic political purposes.

Nevertheless, except on foreign and security policy, British news of the EU is normally little different in volume and focus from that provided in other member states. But tone and emphasis are another issue. British news has a greater component of scepticism and outright hostility than that in any other member state. Some British tabloids especially gave the EU and its institutions a derisive, contemptuous coverage not seen elsewhere. Two case studies give the flavour of such coverage – the BSE crisis of 1996 and the European Parliament elections in 1999.

The BSE crisis of 1996.

The incidence of BSE in British cattle and establishing a link between it and Variant CJD in the UK faced British farming and the food industry with the gravest crisis in living memory. By mid-1996 British beef exports faced a world-wide ban, the possibility of a huge cull of the national herd and draconian controls over abattoirs. The timing could not have been more certain to produce grave embarrassment for the government – and a knee jerk reaction from the British press.

The BSE crisis boosted all EU coverage in the British media. Television coverage rose sharply after February 1996 with agricultural issues averaging nearly three times the EU average at peak times between May and July. Press coverage, already moderately heavy, rose sharply on agricultural, economic, financial, social and health policies to levels noticeably above EU averages, with 30 per cent of the stories being front paged, and 80 per cent focusing on the Commission.

Almost all the coverage exhibited a mix of national anger and exasperation about the crisis and its possible health consequences and, even more, about the responses of EU member governments and EU institutions. The fact that EU experts may already have known about a latent problem and had proposed that EU funds cover most of the cost of the cattle cull thought necessary was lost early in the debate. Some of the coverage hinted that the health threat was exaggerated by member governments anxious to protect their domestic markets against British imports. Xenophobia and paranoia were clearly visible. During most of 1996 only *The Financial Times, The Independent* and *The Guardian* provided sympathetic coverage of EU responses. Coverage elsewhere in the UK suggested that EU events were only news if they held EU up to fierce criticism or even ridicule.

By the spring of 1996 the looming BSE crisis framed virtually all EU coverage. *The Daily Telegraph* on May 23 criticised some MEPs and Commissioner Kinnock for their public doubts about the government's official policy of 'non co-operation' in the EU. On May 31 *The Times* tied the BSE story and government non co-operation to resistance over cuts in fishing quotas. On June 3 *The Daily Telegraph* attacked the leader of the Conservative MEPs, Lord Plumb, as 'pro-German'. By way of contrast *The Independent* concentrated on likely EU assistance in paying for the large cull of British cattle. The newspaper assembled items from the anti-EU press under the title of 'The press crusade for narrow nationalism.' *The Sun* even called for the abolition of the European Parliament and advised its President, Lord Plumb, who was 'nothing more than a jumped up civil servant...to shut up.' *The Financial Times* carried a briefing from Lord Plumb in which he accused British civil servants of overly zealous rule-making, the result of which contributed to the BSE crisis by limiting the number of abattoirs which could undertake the cull. The piece ended with a condescending dismissal of Conservative MEPs from Central Office 'It's pretty lonely being a Tory MEP and they sometimes feel marginalised in the modern Conservative Party. From time to time they make a song and dance about things.' (*Financial Times*, 27 July).

The idea of the European Parliament, including Conservative MEPs, actively criticising British Conservative government policy infuriated the Eurosceptic press – and even more so when the European Parliament set up a full-scale parliamentary investigation into the origins of the BSE scandal. *The Times* and *The Daily Telegraph* countered by 'gravy train' coverage of the Parliament (*Telegraph*, May 22) stressing the costs of MEP expenses and of the new Parliament building in Brussels. *The Times* took the same line in mid-July, noting that each MEP cost £1 million a year to 'keep in business' (*The Times*, 16 July). This appeared just at the moment when the Parliament was trying to tighten the rules governing the MEPs' register of interests.

After the August recess the crisis coverage continued. On September 3 *The Financial Times* reported a leaked Commission memorandum which revealed that in early 1990 the EU's Veterinary Committee concluded 'that it was necessary to minimise the BSE affair by using disinformation.' On September 13 Terry Wynn, a Labour MEP, in a letter in *The Independent,* argued that the decision was a product of EU's secretive, unaccountable committee structure. The following day *The Financial Times* reported that a Commission official had earlier warned of a collapse of beef prices unless the Commission was given power to increase stocks promptly. When, after September 19 the British Cabinet decided not to order a cull of cattle, the Commission retaliated by recommending a continuance of the total ban on British beef exports. Klaus Haensch, the new Parliament President, was quoted in *The Financial Times* as saying that the UK 'did not belong to the Union if it abandoned solidarity.'

Solidarity of sorts there clearly had been. *The Financial Times* on October 2 reported that Guy Legras, the Commission official earlier accused of the EU cover up, denied any such thing. He acknowledged that the EU had feared a consumer panic and argued 'We are trying to manage uncertainty. We are in a huge grey area of doubt.' But a few days later British newspapers returned to the question of the costs of the Parliament and the allegedly fraudulent expense claims of MEPs. President Haensch rejected the allegations of widespread fraud, blaming an 'anti-European campaign by the media in one member state' (*Financial Times,* October 7).

The battle for public opinion continued as the full cost of the BSE crisis emerged. On October 28 *The Financial Times* reported that monies for BSE would have to be found from the cereals support budget. During November the Parliament buzzed with rumours emanating from its Enquiry. On November 27 *The Financial Times* reported that the Enquiry 'left few unscathed' in the Commission, the industry or the veterinary profession. British officials stood to be accused of allowing infected feed to be given to cattle eight years after initial restrictions were in force. The Agriculture Commissioner and Guy Legras were likely to be accused of restricting discussion of BSE to protect beef markets. The Enquiry unearthed conflicts between individuals and Directorates in the Commission. The ban on the export of British gelatine, for example, seemed to have been lifted despite clear scientific evidence of real danger. Parliament's leaders were aware that the Enquiry would boost Parliament's reputation, but they were also aware that the evidence 'could be used by some member states to argue that the Commission's powers should be curbed.' Reimer Boge, a German MEP and the Chair of the Enquiry, was worried that the report 'should not be misused by politicians'. (*Financial Times*, 27 November). The Chair knew that British politicians and the beef and agricultural lobbies would strongly resist such an assertion of Parliamentary influence – and that the British press would be an instrument of that resistance. So it proved.

The coverage of the BSE crisis revealed the patterns of EU decision-making. Clearly there had been a Council decision by governments to avoid consumer panic and protect the EU beef industry. This had involved ignoring scientific evidence and, later, Brussels leaks blaming the British beef industry for the whole matter once the issue went public.

Equally clearly it revealed the pattern of British media coverage. Radio and television strove, at least formally, for dispassionate analysis of the origins and evolution of the BSE crisis. There was sharp criticism but it was usually offset by an awareness of divided expert opinion and political imperatives, not only in the UK but also within and between EU member states and institutions. By contrast a partisan press behaved as expected. The tabloids engaged in anti-EU abuse – items of news which, for them, demonstrated the need either to refashion the EU or withdraw from it. The anti-EU broadsheets put the same points without the abuse and, more circumspectly, portrayed the British government as only a little more guilty than other members of the EU. The pro-EU press did the reverse, blaming the British government more than it probably deserved and largely ignoring evidence critical of the EU's role and that of other member governments. It was not an edifying episode in British journalism and probably as much coloured by the coming general election as by specific BSE claims, counterclaims and tragedies. The exception was *The Financial Times* which, as a committed and respected pro-EU newspaper, was the chosen vehicle for the Commission and parliamentary leaderships to try to put on record the complex truths of the whole matter.

European Parliament Elections 1999

British media coverage of the election exemplified the kind of treatment of EU subjects which enrages Brussels officials. At the very start a low turnout was predicted and the coverage mirrored electoral disinterest. Television and radio covered very little of the campaign. Only in the last few days could the election be said to have been given any prominence in the media. Low expectations bred weak interest.

The press followed a similar pattern and behaved predictably. Among the broadsheets *The Guardian* in a May 31 item headed 'Don't Yawn for Europe – Apathy must not win elections' urged voters to turn out and two days later noted that 'Labour set for big losses.' A week later *The Guardian* returned to the election. Its veteran correspondent Michael White's column was headlined 'Victory for apathy feared.' The same day his colleague Martin Walker noted 'A bizarre equation is under way in which the more democratic Europe's institutions become, the less the voters cast their ballots.' The following day another colleague Polly Toynbee noted that '...anti-European resentment has risen ominously [&] saving William Hague to lose the next election may suit Labour, but letting his anti-European rhetoric rip is doing serious damage.' On election day Hugo Young blamed the likely low turnout on the failure of politicians to lead – 'consigned into murk, the electorate takes the only vengeance available and withdraws from the operation.' That same day an editorial headed 'Vote if you are still awake' noted that 'The impression has grown that Labour wanted this not to be a midterm referendum on its performance.' Labour MPs, the newspaper argued, who were afraid of proportional representation (PR) want this ' lukewarm result ' blamed on PR.

For a stoutly pro-EU newspaper *The Independent* did not offer very much enthusiasm before election day. On June 2 it offered an item headed 'MEPs win bonuses in perks cutback' and followed this with 'One black MP for all Europe' – neither item calculated to stir mass enthusiasm. On the morning of the election it featured a piece entitled 'What election? A big vote for apathy' – this being one of three pieces presumably aimed at getting pro-EU voters out to vote. *The Financial Times*' British edition was curiously mute before the elections, though noting the widespread public apathy in a resigned tone. Not surprisingly *The Glasgow Herald* and *The Scotsman* were both concerned over the possibility of losing EU finance for Scotland. Scottish MEPs had been influential inside the Labour Party delegation in Parliament and had been purged by the Blairites in the reselection process – a fact *The Glasgow Herald* alluded to in a June 3 piece headed 'Honourable MEPs?' Among the tabloids the pro-EU *Daily Mirror* had the most urgent coverage. On June 3 a piece headed 'Why Europe matters to us' urged voters to turn out and vote and this was echoed in an item by Neil Kinnock on June 7.

Not surprisingly those newspapers sceptical or hostile to many aspects of the EU had a field day, especially as election day approached. Among the broadsheets *The Daily Telegraph* was the most hostile. On May 31 it ran a piece entitled 'PR robs voters of right to pick their local MP.' Ten days later, on the eve of the election its correspondent Toby Helm had a piece headed 'Like it or loathe it – Brussels does matter.' This argued that the Parliament was important 'As power is sucked away from national governments to European institutions, much of it is ending up in the hands of 626 Europe MPs.' He went on: '80 per cent of the legislation concerning the environment now originates in Brussels. Soon the proportion will be similar in other areas.' An editorial headed 'Vote Tory Today' provided the reasons: 'Vote against cronyism, corruption, farming damage, fishing ground damage, Working Time Directive, end of duty free, qualified majority voting, harmonisation of taxes and criminal justice, no European army.'

The Times coverage was little different. On June 2 an editorial 'Pounding Labour' noted Robin Cook's rejection of William Hague's choice of the euro as the campaign focus and added 'It is for the electorate to decide whether or not they agree with him.' A news item the same day noted without enthusiasm the large number of women candidates in the election. On June 7 Peter Riddell's column was headed 'Labour's Missed Opportunity'. It criticised the complacency of Labour's campaign, welcomed the effective Tory campaign, and added: 'Some Labour people want the Tories to do well to ensure that Mr.

Hague remains a Leader.' He noted, however, that the Tories seemed to want 'a big single market and free trading area preferably enlarged across the Atlantic but without any other obligations or rules.' A news item the same day referred to MEPs as 'retreads' and in an editorial the newspaper urged 'Vote on Thursday – unless you think the EU needs no improvement.' On election day, June 10, *The Times* urged voters to vote: 'You've got the power.' The tabloids did not match the coverage offered by the broadsheets prior to the election – possibly because the Kosovo crisis provided an alternative focus which they could not ignore. Both *The Daily Express* and *Daily Mail* noted the apathy among voters but did not subsequently provide much guidance for voters. Perhaps each, independently, had decided that silence was golden,

The election results were not declared officially until Sunday June 13 and the response from the media was predictable. Radio and television news carried the overall results and noted that, despite prior discounting, Labour ministers were publicly disappointed. They reported that in private they were very angry at the party's failure to campaign to get the vote out. The Tories, of course, were reported to be much heartened by a gain of 34 seats, seeing it as a vindication of scepticism toward the EU and an endorsement of William Hague's position as Leader.

Newspapers responded appropriately. *The Guardian* repeated the Tory claim that the result vindicated Mr. Hague, and stressed the low turnout and a worrying EU-wide trend against the Third Way. A piece by Ewen MacAskill and Lucy Ward criticised both government ministers and Labour Party headquarters for not giving a lead. They noted that 'British and German socialists are the biggest losers.' That was the context, they said, in which Hague's 'scepticism' paid off.

In contrast *The Independent* was eloquent. Andrew Grice on June 14 noted that the results showed the government's message had been more 'focused on Middle England than on the working class' who were less pro-EU than the leadership. He went on to note trenchantly: 'These results blow a hole in the Blairite claim that our people have nowhere else to go – they can stay at home.' Peter Mandelson, he thought, should be recalled to head the campaign organisation. The following day a reinforcing message came from Peter Kellner -'Why Labour can't blame voter fatigue, contentment or PR', and next day from Berlin Imre Kovacs drew parallels with the election in Germany, adding 'The Third Way is no longer an election winner.'

The Financial Times, which had had little to say before the election, quoted psephologist Professor Anthony King to the effect that 'the Labour vote has simply imploded' and added that neither Blair nor Hague had shown real leadership. The newspaper's viewpoint was given by Peter Norman, the Brussels correspondent, who argued that the result might have a silver lining in that the low turnout reduced the Parliament's legitimacy making it 'a less abrasive assembly.' Clutching at straws seemed to be the order of the day.

The Conservative anti-EU press was delighted with the result. In *The Daily Telegraph* George Jones crowed in a piece headlined 'Tories trounce Labour in Europe' while Toby Helm's piece was headlined 'Apathy rules in the great European stay away poll.' The following day Anthony King under the headline 'Why Labour is looking old hat' noted that Labour supporters were 'alienated in large numbers.' The same day *The Times* carried a piece by Tim Hames arguing that Hague's gamble had paid off: 'It is Ashdown, Clark and Heseltine who are the losers' since Hague's position had been secured. The following day Hames returned with a warning that 'Tories must beware of the sting in the tail', arguing that Hague was still unpopular in key marginal seats and that Labour ministers now realised just how bad PR would be for them. This was a lesson not lost on certain members of the Cabinet 'who would see that the first past the post system was biased in favour of Labour.' In an editorial the Prime Minister was urged to put aside 'abstract constitutional ideas, back door coalition bargains, proportional representation and the drive for European integration.' In the same issue Peter Riddell noted that Labour voters had not seen the benefits of Blairism and concluded that 'Labour's poor results were as much a warning about domestic as European politics.'

The tabloids were clear that the election results constituted a referendum on Europe. *The Daily Mail* editorialised on June 15 claiming that Conservatives 'campaigned anti-euro. They won anti-euro.' In the same issue Stephen Glover, under a headline 'So Hague's not so vague after all' noted that Conservatives had united against the euro and won. He then went on to criticise the Liberal Democrat leader, Paddy Ashdown, as 'off beam...In case he hasn't noticed, most British people are opposed to the introduction of the euro and the inevitable further political integration that would follow.'

The Daily Express preferred to highlight the reshuffle of Hague's Shadow Cabinet. Columnist Anthony Bevins noted on June 16 how, in sacking Peter Lilley, Gillian Shepherd, Norman Fowler and Michael Howard, the Leader had used Europe to 'get a tighter grip on the Party including a take-over of the policy review.' The newspaper, however, editorialised 'New Faces do not a new Party make' in which it asserted that being anti-euro was not enough – 'more is needed.' Andrew Marr in the same issue provided a similar analysis and a series of suggestions for Prime Minister Tony Blair. Primarily these were 'Forget the euro' and abandon any further 'tinkering with the Constitution.' 'Blair,' he said, 'must stop being a victim of the advice of friends.'

Some emphasis in the press coverage stressed the danger to Labour's standing rather than the importance of reducing a perceived 'democratic deficit' in Europe. The coverage after the election noted Labour's continued 20 point lead in opinion polls, exuded little enthusiasm for the European Parliament or EU generally, and interpreted the elections as a discounted negative blip in the progress of a successful Labour government heading for an inevitable second term. True, election coverage after election day urged Tony Blair to 'get out and sell Labour achievements'. In pro-EU papers, selling the EU was added as an achievement. The anti-EU newspapers chose to interpret the results as a decisive rejection of further EU integration, even a rejection of the EU itself.

The validity or otherwise of these press judgements is not here in question – but the tone is only too obviously illustrative. The results had little by way of immediate political consequence – a second Labour term in office in Britain seemed assured. But they reflected in the media the deep divisions in popular opinion and between the parties on the issue of Europe.

Conclusions

The British media is caught like a fly in aspic as far as reporting Europe is concerned. Little has changed over a number of years for the British press corps in Brussels. The newspaper culture in London is still highly partisan on the EU and journalists build that into their reporting. A 1999 analysis by Stephen Bales—'Brussels with the blinkers on' stressed the degree of misunderstanding and scare stories still visible in the British press. The European Commission Office in London publishes a regular Press Watch which lists examples. Such coverage makes it difficult to stage a quality debate on the whole EMU-EU question.

The British press corps in Brussels may have grown more unpopular among officials because its abrasion appears to be spreading to journalists from other countries. Certainly deference to political leaders and political parties in member states is visibly in decline as revelations of party 'slush funds' in Germany and France encourage such investigations elsewhere. In-depth reports on problems such as the fluctuating value of the euro and the difficulties of framing an immigration policy get little exposure alongside scandal and sleaze. Political leaders in all member states are on notice that loyalty and deference among journalists are in short supply and that the elite consensus on European integration is much weakened. Jacques Delors conceded as much more than five years ago but the message is slow to be appreciated more widely. A changing culture among continental journalists must reflect both changing realities in Brussels and expectations among their domestic audiences. Up to a point reporters could ignore the former, but not the latter.

In addition there are questions around the presentation of EU news. As additional sources such as interest groups have proliferated in Brussels, so it has become more difficult for EU institutions and member governments to manage EU news in ways that applied hitherto. This has had two results. Commissioners and Directorates have become more concerned with presentation and some have grown notably more secretive. Journalists, in something of a reaction to this, have become even more sceptical and are more prepared to go outside official sources in the Commission and Council to look more to interest groups and lobbyists. Even their own governments may be more ready to divulge off-the-record information to strengthen their hands in Council or in the European Parliament. The news management battle is thus sharpening up as both sides grasp its full import. As in the US, so in the EU, the 'real news' for good reporters is increasingly sought in a multiplicity of sources and not simply from official spokespersons and institutions.

Thus, finally, EU coverage in the future is likely to see some significant changes as it reflects changing political realities in Brussels and within member states. So long as member governments find it convenient, the Council will continue to be a secretive and difficult news source for journalists. It is, after all, the arena for resolving conflicts over policies and this, inevitably, will involve implicit and explicit governmental agreements which could be deeply embarrassing should they be revealed. Likewise the Commission will seek to be more coherent in its presentation of news, all the while being less than transparent when political necessity demands that. The European Parliament will continue to be covered as it has been until it comes into acute conflict with Commission and Council. Most of its coverage will continue to be of individual members rather than the institution, and it will continue to be a vehicle for local demands. It is sedulously cultivating better media coverage and it intends a more challenging role toward both the Commission and the Council. Eastward expansion of the Union can only strengthen demands by members to lessen the 'democratic deficit'.

The result is an EU image which seems to consist of an overly powerful unelected Commission and an elected but ineffective Parliament – neither representing the full truth of the situation. Recently Karl Heinz Neunreither characterised the European Parliament elections as 'more or less a test of popularity of the national government.' What is needed, he argued, is 'a real European agenda….an opportunity to vote for names and personalities, if possible not just of senior MEPs, but candidates for the Commission as well.' (Government and Opposition, Vol.33, No. 4).

Rhetoric apart, national electorates and their governments are divided on yielding ever more powers of decision to a Union of states, far less anything that might resemble a so-called 'European superstate'. The uncertain progress of the Constitutional Convention has shown this and the current Intergovernmental Conference may yet decide not to endorse the progressive steps the Convention suggested. Media coverage in most member states partially conceals or distorts these doubts and uncertainties while not increasing the levels of public knowledge. Media coverage, however, cannot be said of itself to create basic conflicts though, improperly presented, it can make national and inter-governmental debates more difficult. It may well be that the UK profile of media coverage, in its sins of omission and commission, exemplifies a deepening problem as the EU seeks both increased integration and eastward expansion.

British Press Coverage of Europe
Jim Dougal

Ever since the UK joined the Common Market in 1973, tales have abounded of an overweening bureaucracy attempting to rest control of Britain into its own hands. Continual warnings of 'barmy EU edicts' issued by 'faceless eurocrats', which have surreptitiously impinged upon British life to deleterious effect, have been the mainstay of EU reporting in much of the UK press. Indeed, were every portentous prediction to have come to fruition, we would now be living in a kind of Orwellian dystopia, with many aspects of British life, from the minutiae to the monumental, pre-ordained by the abstract monolith known as 'Brussels'.

We would be driving along roads with alien numbers: E30, E73, E92. Roads no longer lined with hedgerows full of British wildlife – these having been pulled down by farmers to increase their Common Agricultural Policy subsidies. Instead, busts of Jacques Delors would adorn our highways. We would see grocers carted off to jail for selling non-straight cucumbers and overly-bent bananas. Playgrounds would be left desolate – swings and slides having been torn down at the behest of EU pen pushers. Piling the grief on children, treasured household pets could no longer be given a proper burial unless their bodies had first been boiled in pressure-cookers.

Even a visit to the local pub for a litre of beer would be prohibited unless regulation earmuffs were worn to protect against excessive noise from music or chatter. Ordering cod and chips would have to be done in Latin because of the confusion caused to foreigners by the use of

English. Feeding the ducks during a stroll in the park would be illegal unless you possessed a licence to distribute waste food. The recipient ducks would need one, too.

Clearly none of the above myths, in common with the vast majority of others, have come to pass as reality in the UK. What *has* become all too real is the indelible impression of the EU left on the public conscience by this constant trickle of prevarication. The cumulative effect of this kind of journalism has certainly had a hugely damaging effect on the EU's reputation within the UK. Regrettably, such an admission will be interpreted as a receipt of success for many.

As Britain marks the 30th anniversary of its membership of the European Community, this culture of misrepresentation still infuses press coverage of EU affairs. The reasons for this still-prevalent euroscepticism across the UK has many origins, ranging from the historical to thinly-veiled xenophobia, and from ignorance as well as considered economic and political analysis. Undoubtedly, the most viable and effective apparatus for expression of this panorama of europhobic opinion has been via euromyths, which are, at best, grotesque caricatures of the truth or simply pure invention of what the EU is about. By distortion and invention they are designed to belittle, ridicule or horrify, depending on the subject matter and the audience.

The event which was singularly most generative of these euromyths was the creation of the internal market. The Single European Act of 1986 set a deadline of 1992 for the single market to become operational. Inherent in the establishment of this level playing field for inter-EU trade was the harmonisation of national laws. Despite this hugely complex legislative process being administered with flexibility and sensitivity to member states' national proclivities, it proved a fertile source of euromyths.

Platforms for dissatisfaction

Although much of the legislation merely reaffirmed national measures already in place, the misperception of the EU covertly pervading every aspect of everyday life was seized upon. The introduction of common marketing and labelling standards for foodstuffs in particular – 'straight cucumbers' and 'bent bananas' being the most iconoclastic examples – proved a malleable source for misrepresentation, and remains so today, as evidenced by a recent story that mince pies were about to be banned. Subsequently, the lengthy and troubled ratification of the Maastricht Treaty in 1993 provided the ideal platform for expressions of dissatisfaction towards the EU. The withdrawal of the whip from nine Conservative MPs, and their subsequent media ubiquity during this period, gave the eurosceptic camp an impetus that was further fuelled by the Major government's vulnerability because of its small majority in the Commons. The prosaic terminology used by the then Prime Minister for the 'Maastricht rebels' and others sealed their status as adopted figureheads within the eurosceptic press, and the prominence of the story was such that it was impossible for the more measured media to ignore. The ever-present politico-media mix was distilled into a lethal eurosceptic cocktail. The press could get away with almost any rubbish about the European Union.

Various ways of combating this were established. One of the most longlasting has proved to be Press Watch, first published in 1996 as an attempt (for that was all it could be) by the European Commission in the UK to counter this collusion of agenda-driven misrepresentation and inaccuracy. Sent out to MPs, peers, the newspapers themselves and other 'opinion-formers', this periodic publication – now in its seventh year and heading towards its sixteenth issue – catalogues recent euromyths; not all, but those that have been most widely covered in the newspapers. The knee-jerk reaction most often levied at Press Watch is that the Commission – as one MP's correspondence recently put it – should be using its resources to deal with the 'real issues of substance and concern'. After all, the EU is currently undergoing an unprecedented enlargement process, with all the political, social, and economic extrapolations this entails, including reform of the organisation's institutions. Further major changes have been necessitated within the agricultural and fisheries sectors, and the euro has just celebrated its first anniversary. Unfortunately, for much of the media it is not these 'real issues of substance and concern' that are of interest- it is the banning of lemon curd, swings, islands, and church bells, along with the provision of toys for pigs. My office has to deal with the situation as it finds it.

As with all political institutions, the EU must have its workings and policies brought to light and subjected to vigorous scrutiny by the media. Even the most ardent europhile would concede that there is ample scope for constructive, considered criticism. But if the agenda that spawns euromyths is that membership of the EU is of such damaging consequence to the UK, then surely there are more cogent arguments to be postulated than those concerning the size of peaches and the banning of corgis? If the eurosceptic argument is so strong, why does the need for insidious invention remain?

The point is often made that my office should utilise the Press Complaints Commission to respond to such articles, but it has proved an impractical and inefficient course to pursue. On the one occasion this route was taken, the protracted negotiations with both the PCC and the newspaper concerned, and the subsequent result, were both unsatisfactory. We pursued a case following a three-tier headline, double-page article in *The Mail on Sunday* which contained a panoply of lies and misinformation on a Commission-run shop. After two months of frustrating negotiations with first, as required, the newspaper concerned, and subsequently the PCC, the upshot was the publication of a desultorily small correction and a rebuttal letter – a result diluted by its retrospection and hardly an adequate counterbalance to the impact of the initial article.

Yet it is not merely the logistical impediments that impair the effectiveness of the PCC, but the whole ethos behind the watchdog. A key tenet of the PCC's claims for self-regulation of the press is that the Code derives its strength because it is set and applied by those who must abide by it, i.e. the newspapers themselves. The PCC's website claims that 'self regulation works because the newspaper and magazine publishing industry is committed to it'. Thus, in theory, self-regulation produces an industry that holds the Code in such reverence that the veracity of stories is exhaustively researched, and corrections and letters of rebuttal willingly printed upon recognition of a 'significant inaccuracy, misleading statement, or distorted report'. The actuality however, as experienced by my office, is substantially different.

Wilful ignorance

A spate of stories earlier this year was an object lesson in not 'taking care' to establish the accuracy of facts before publication. Indeed, in many cases, it was apparent that this requirement was flagrantly overlooked, as even the most ephemeral of inquiries would have made it impossible to run the stories. This wilful ignorance is never more apparent than when the EU is taken as a generic term to cover anything vaguely European or based in Brussels. An all-embracing knowledge of European institutions is not a requisite of accurate reporting, but surely being able to identify basic political distinctions is? In 1996, the very first issue of Press Watch featured a leader column in the *Daily Express* on the European Court of Human Rights, which stated:

> 'It is time Ministers explained why Britain, unlike Germany, does not have a simple constitutional clause asserting that British law will always take primacy over those emanating from the European Union and its institutions.'

A mantra often repeated by my staff is that the European Court of Human Rights is a body of the Council of Europe, an intergovernmental organisation entirely separate from the EU. Eight years on and this same distortion of fact to implicate the EU in stories with which it has no connection remains steadfastly employed by journalists. In a recent article in *The Daily Telegraph* entitled 'Church bells silenced by fear of EU law' it transpired that the copy referred to the European Convention on Human Rights. Again, this is a body of law derived from the Council of Europe, not the EU.

This was further evidenced in the various stories concerning the demolition of a set of playground swings. According to the reports, a local council, in response to EU law, had been forced to demolish a set of swings because they did not conform to the legislation concerned. Among the emotive headlines used was the *Daily Express's* cod-exasperated 'You could just swing for them! – EU officials shut playground favourite', and *The Time's* confidently assertive 'Children pushed off swings by EU'. Suitably lachrymose pictures of the children affected were used to further illustrate the terrible effect of EU law. Ostensibly another classic case of EU meddling; in reality, the whole affair was based around an entirely voluntary measure, set by a non-EU body, and already adopted by the British Standards Institute some years ago. But because the relevant body, the European Standardisation Committee, contained that generic affirmation of nuisance, 'European', the stories ran with the EU firmly positioned in the role of villain.

When attempting to rebut these stories, whether through letters for publication or to editors, the production of Press Watch, or via contact with individual journalists, my office is confronted with a combination of obduracy, often based around semantic obfuscation, and incredulity. Witness one conversation between a member of our press office who, on telling a *Daily Express* journalist that her story on alleged EU laws on street lighting was wrong, was met with the response: 'Well, the EU meddles into (sic) all sorts of areas, so it wouldn't surprise me if this was true'.

Even in instances of acknowledged factual inaccuracy there remains an unwillingness to publish letters of correction, and when this concession is granted, the correspondence often appears in edited form and is given little prominence – certainly in relation to the original stories to which they refer. When confronted over such articles, the prevailing attitude among the press seems to be that they cannot believe the EU has the temerity to respond to any allegations, however spurious. In the case of stories that I would readily agree are of a humorous nature, as opposed to those that are laughable, the accusation is levelled that the Commission is being po-faced for considering them worthy of refutation. Against a backdrop of consistently objective criticism of the EU and non-prejudicial coverage of EU affairs, it would be plausible to accept them as innocuously frivolous. When they constitute such a vast proportion of coverage, to the extent that the public perception of the EU has irrefutably come to be defined in such limited terms, they cannot he treated so magnanimously.

Worst exponents

There is simply no incentive for newspapers to check their facts before running an inaccurate eurosceptic story. The concept of the PCC's code of practice and self-control via self-regulation being an inducement to accuracy is anathema to the reality. In its stead is the journalistic complacency that derives from being untouchable and unaccountable, two accusations that are readily directed towards the institutions of the EU. This, when mingled with the type of editorialising copy – again in complete violation of the Code – seen in so-called news stories ('...the cretins in land-locked Brussels...' *Daily Mail,* 24 January), somewhat contradicts the grandiose claim of the PCC that 'self-regulation combines high standards of ethical reporting with a free press'. Rather, it certainly guarantees the latter, while legitimising fabrication via the comfortable charade of supposed adherence to the Code.

The correlation between the national newspapers represented on the PCC's Code of Practice Committee and those that are the worst exponents of europhobic pretence is too striking to engender confidence in the current system. But even with a more rigorous application of the principles of self-regulation it would be unlikely that the current trend of reporting of EU affairs would alter dramatically. With political procrastination over the UK's role in Europe and a media pandering to the baser nationalistic interests of its readership, there can be no serious basis for discussion. Until stronger political leadership indicates that Britain is committed to fulfilling its role as a vital partner within the EU, there can be no expectation of a higher standard of coverage of EU affairs.

Note

This article is reprinted by kind permission of Sage Publications Ltd. from *British Journalism Review*. Copyright BJR Publishing Ltd.

Priorities in Information Policy
Roy Perry MEP

Is there a European information policy?

By almost any measure, after 45 years of its existence in one form or another, the European Union is barely understood by the average citizen and still less appreciated.

I have no doubt that the information policy of the European Parliament, in so far as it has an information policy, has achieved a near total failure with respect to explaining the work of the European Union. From the UK's perspective, it has been a total failure.

It is amazing that whilst one half of Europe is queuing up to join the EU, and other countries such as Turkey seem to be deeply disappointed that they cannot yet join the Union, those peoples currently in the Union, have no overwhelming enthusiasm for the organisation that the Union has become. The few exceptions, such as Belgians and Luxemburgers, hardly affect the general conclusion, and that despite an unrivalled period of peace and prosperity which has coincided for most states with European Union membership.

If there is a policy, is it working?

According to the Eurobarometer of Spring 2002 only 28 per cent of respondents knew much about the EU and only 2 out of 10 said they took much notice of information about the EU. Turnout across the Union for the European Parliament elections has fallen from 63 per cent in 1979 to 49 per cent in the 1999 elections, descending to the depths of the poor turnout we see in American presidential elections.

According to almost all main indicators some 50 per cent of the citizens are ignorant or indifferent to the Union. This ignorance or indifference – and the corresponding danger to the Union – was brilliantly summed up in the anti-Euro slogan in the Irish Euro referendum. *'If you don't know, vote No.'* There is a risk of this injunction becoming the public's reaction towards the EU as a whole.

The high ideals of the founding fathers to establish a better way for Europe to order its affairs than the methods of the first half of the 20th century and earlier – which was the central motivation of the EU - have now seemingly descended into a morass of detailed rules and regulations, apocryphally thought to be more concerned with the curvature of bananas and the length of cucumbers than anything of greater importance. The fact that consumers are able to buy and afford as many good quality bananas or cucumbers as they wish, whenever they wish, is lost in the popular perception that the EU is somehow interfering in this process rather than facilitating it.

An experience of my own in my constituency of South East England demonstrates the scale of the problem in a morbid manner. I was contacted by my constituency party office to say that they had been telephoned by a deeply distressed gentleman. His wife had just died and her great wish had been that she should be cremated. However, the local crematorium had said that this was not possible as she required a 32 inch wide coffin but coffins of that size were prohibited by EU regulations which limited coffins to a width of 2 inches. I ought to have been immediately suspicious, since an EU rule would have been in metric measure. However, I telephoned the director of the crematorium to enquire into the problem and to see if there was any way to help my constituent in his deep and genuine distress. The crematorium director immediately knew whom I was speaking about and the circumstances of the case. 'No', he admitted, 'there is no EU regulation. It is simply that the diameter of the crematorium furnace door is 30 inches. This means we limit a coffin to 27 inches which allows an inch either side for passing the coffin into the furnace, with an inch for luck!' I particularly appreciated that need for the final inch, which struck a genuine and typically English note. The director said he knew the undertaker concerned, whom he said was a kind man, who would not want to cause any offence to a grieving family by telling them the deceased was simply too fat to be cremated. So, he invented the excuse of a mythical EU regulation. Just blame Brussels!

It may seem a harmless story perhaps, and no fault of the EU, one might think. The problem, however, is two-fold. 'Brussels' has become an easy and remote scapegoat for any mishap, leading to more and more such stories and a jaundiced opinion of EU rules and regulations. But the real problem for the Union, and its responsibility as well, is that people are ready to believe such stories, no matter how absurd they may be.

As a member of the European Parliament's Culture Committee since 1994, the Committee which has responsibility for information policy, I must accept a degree of responsibility for this lamentable state of affairs.

Are there too many information policies and too many cooks in the kitchen?

The latest report adopted by the Culture Committee in February 2003 on information and communication policy for the European Union is that of Senor Juan Josè Bayona de Perogordo. In his report he cites no fewer than nineteen similar reports, going back as far as a resolution of 15 February 1957 on 'informing public opinion about the activity of the Community'. More recent reports he referred to included the EP Bureau decision of April 2001 on interinstitutional co-operation in the field of communication and information policy and a resolution of March 2002 on the Commission communication on a new framework for co-operation on activities concerning the information and communication policy of the European Union. There has clearly been no shortage of thought and debate on information and communication policy, nor players ready to become involved, but effectiveness and consistency is quite another matter.

Immediately one can see a problem. There is no clear single body or person responsible for information policy. Furthermore, one all important body, namely the Council of Ministers, is rather distant from the process. Within the Commission, responsibility seems to be confusingly shared between two Commissioners, Commission President

Roman Prodi and Commissioner Vitorino. The Commissioner responsible for Culture had this responsibility stripped away at the start of this five year term of office. So the Commissioner who most regularly comes to the Culture Committee, which retains responsibility within parliamentary terms of reference, is not the Commissioner actually responsible for information policy. Commissioner Vitorino is expected to cover this role as an 'add on' to his main responsibility for Justice and Home Affairs.

If the UK office of the Commission is typical of the work in member states, despite sterling work by the very limited number of officials, these offices do not regard their role as being apologists for or proponents of the EU. Rather as a dedicated treasurer who accurately and carefully records a growing deficit, they will carefully report back to Brussels the scale of the problem but do not see it as their responsibility to adopt a proactive role. Nor do they have the resources to perform such a role.

Commission President Prodi, who famously described the rules of the economic stability pact as 'stupid', does not seem to have a clear grasp of the basic rules of any information policy, nor to have sought to attract into the Commission services any professional expertise. The Commission, that has only recently thought it necessary to have an accountant in charge of its accounts, has yet to consider it necessary to have any professional PR personnel for its PR policy, or even to appoint overall PR consultants.

Within parliamentary terms there are also lots of fingers officially in the pie, as well as other less official fingers. The Bureau of Parliament appoints a Vice-President with responsibility for information policy. Successively they seem to carry out this role with scant regard for the work of the Culture Committee.

The information offices of the Parliament in the member states come under the direct supervision of the College of Quaestors and it is far from clear what consideration is given to PR experience or expertise in appointing the heads of these offices. From my experience the offices do a good job in responding to enquiries and maintaining liaison with public authorities, but whether they are given a brief to be pro-active in an increasingly hostile or agnostic climate I am less sure. I can re-call no report on appointments to these crucial positions or the processes involved and the qualities sought ever being presented to the Culture Committee, and yet these officers are in the front line of information policy.

The Culture Committee has nominal responsibility for information and communication policy and writes reports on the issue with monotonous regularity, but who actually reads these reports and whether anything is ever done about their (often nebulous) conclusions is far from clear.

The Budgets Committee of the Parliament is another player on the scene and increases or decreases the sums allocated to information and communication policy at will, and again with scant regard for the views and deliberations of the Culture Committee or the Bureau.

Democracy has never been described as the most efficient form of government, but paradoxically one could argue that, if one wanted to see an efficient communication and information policy, one could only wish that the democratic deficit that is said to exist in the EU were far greater than it actually is.

Should the press be expected to be fair and impartial?

The European Union's communication and information policy does not exist in a neutral climate. In Britain, whilst the press cannot be described as universally hostile to the Union, it gives every indication of being overwhelmingly so. An extremely interesting book, '*Insulting the Public: The British Press and the European Union*' has been written by Peter J. Anderson and Anthony Weymouth. This carefully analyses the way in which the European Union and issues relating to it are represented to the public. It asks the question: will biased and negative reporting on the EU help undermine long term stability and security in Europe as some have claimed? I think its conclusions are important, and it certainly shows the climate in which the EU is dealt with by the British press.

Of course, newspaper editors would say they seek to represent the concerns of their readers and that they reflect opinion rather than shape it. But if that were indeed the case, why would commercial interests pay considerable sums to place paid advertisements in the press or why would commercial publicists go to extraordinary lengths to place favourable stories in the press? That there is a limit to how far you can spin a story is undoubtedly the case. But that spin or distortion has no effect at all on public opinion seems to me to be just as far from reality. At some stage since the referendum of 1975, when the British press was overwhelmingly in favour of a *Yes* vote, a decision was taken by many newspapers to adopt positions critical if not openly hostile to the Union. The Christopher Booker column in the Sunday Telegraph is a good example of this approach. It may be in part that this change in position by the press could be because the Union itself has changed – which indeed it has as it has developed from EEC to EU – but are the EU's aims so different from the organisation for which *The Times, Sun, Mail, Telegraph* urged a *Yes* vote in the referendum?

It is worth recalling the following statements from various tabloid and broadsheet newspapers. *The Sun* on the 4th June 1975,

'You can vote YES – FOR A FUTURE TOGETHER
Or NO – FOR A FUTURE ALONE
And what have they lost? Sovereignty? Rubbish!
Are the French a soupçon less French?
Are the Germans a sauerkraut less German?
Are the Italians a pizza less Italian?
OF COURSE THEY ARE NOT!
And neither would Britain be any less British',
'The whole history of our nation is a history of absorbing, and profiting by, any European influences that blow our way'.

The Daily Mail on the same day lead with: 'The anti-marketeers have a glum lack of faith in Britain's ability to hold her own inside the market – coupled with an unremitting suspicion of foreigners'.

The Daily Telegraph on the 5th June said:

The Daily Telegraph is increasingly convinced, by the relentless course of daily events, that Western Europe's integration is mandatory for its survival and prosperity in the face of the mounting Soviet threat and other cataclysmic changes in the military, political and economic pattern of world affairs. In the age of super-powers and nuclear weapons, political unity is Europe's only key to security...the present European Communities, with their framework for compromise and common action, are the only means to the laying of just hands on that golden key...the integration of foreign policies must go hand in hand with that of defence policies. With equal logic both must be combined with the integrated economic policy which is already blazing the trail'.

On the 7th May, it welcomed the result by saying:

'Now that the decision has been so clearly taken, it will be up to everyone to make a success of it. This means that Britain will have to throw herself wholeheartedly into improving the institutions and workings of the community...it is a goal, when we have long lacked one. Defence, foreign affairs, economics must all be harnessed to the task of strengthening Europe, and by so doing, strengthening Britain. If this is our approach, the welcome from the European Partners will be warm. We shall help ourselves and them!

It seems to me that in 1975 they understood the situation very well. Was the EEC ever a mere free trade area as is sometimes now claimed? If the EEC were only a free trade area, why did we not join in 1957 but instead set up the rival European Free Trade Area in 1958? When Britain wound up EFTA to join the EEC in 1973, it was clear we were joining up to something other than a mere free trade area. I have never heard a friend or a critic describe the Common Agricultural Policy, for instance, as merely free trade. Are we to believe that the press as well as the public was somehow duped by this? Of course, it may be the move from 'common market' to 'single market' – enacted by the Single Europe Act of 1986 – that led to the change of opinion. But the bulk of the press very much welcomed that move as a way to promote increased intra-union trade and bring about increased prosperity, recognising it would be the inevitable result of increased harmonisation of trade rules.

But change of mind in the media there undoubtedly has been, and it is the proprietors and editors who must answer for that. *The Daily Telegraph* now openly questions the case for British membership of the EU, and its proprietor has advocated British membership of the North American Free Trade Area instead of the EU. Things have come to a pretty pass.

For EU information policy, the reality that has to be borne in mind is that, in Britain at least, there is a daily drip feed of stories hostile to the EU. One would need to read very closely and look very hard for the last time the bulk of the press published even a single positive story about the EU. EU press officers have a tough job and need to bear in mind that their stories are not landing on the desks or computer screens of impartial editors.

Does the EU have a policy of instant rebuttal of false stories? If so, it is not working. There have been attempts by the Commission at publishing booklets rebutting the so-called 'euro-myths'. But by the time editions of these booklets are published, the myth is well established and believed to be the truth. Belated attempts at rebuttal simply give additional publicity to the story and create additional opportunity for elements of the press to rubbish the EU. Who reads these rebuttal booklets, anyway?

After more than 10 years of this daily criticism, it is a wonder that anybody can be found in Britain who supports the EU. Similarly, in the light of this press climate it remains surprising that the official policy of the three major parties remains committed to membership of the EU. Even the most sceptical Conservative Party fought the last European Parliament elections on a slogan and manifesto committed to *'IN EUROPE, NOT RUN BY EUROPE'*. As a pro-European Conservative MEP, I sometimes wonder just how long my party will retain its commitment to British membership of the EU. We shall no doubt see shortly in the manifesto for the 2004 European Parliament elections, and it could be a close-run thing.

Since the correspondence columns of the national and regional press – as well as the saloon bar debate in the 'Dog and Duck' – present a very one- sided debate, one suspects that some Tory strategists, not to mention MPs and MEPs, would welcome a move to outright opposition to British membership of the EU. Being in long-term opposition can indeed be liberating – but does detach one from reality.

In this generally hostile media context it is an open question whether the President of the Commission has an efficient and ruthless Director of Communications. Does Romano Prodi have an equivalent of Alistair Campbell? He certainly needs one, and preferably fifteen of them to cope with each national audience in the Union.

Do we yet have TV in Europe without frontiers?

Television has long been the major source of information for most people on all public affairs, and consequently a strategy for TV reporting of the EU should be a major priority as 98 per cent of EU households are now equipped with a television set.

In most member states, television has more of a reputation for objectivity and neutrality than the press. One cannot but suspect that one of the reasons for the increasing litany of press and political attacks on the BBC in Britain is because the BBC reports EU issues in a manner that is not always negative.

Both the European Parliament and the Commission have impressive television facilities and readily make these available to national broadcasting companies. It is less apparent whether good use is made of these facilities. The Europe by Satellite facility costs 6 million euro a year – a significant part of the information budget – but it is not easy to discover how much of its footage is actually taken by broadcasters in the member states, and how it is used. The Green Group in the EP has learned the tactic of mounting stunts in the chamber to get TV coverage, whether it be opposition to French nuclear tests or war in Iraq, but the Commission and Parliament in general have a very pedestrian way of putting over their message in what is after all a visual medium.

The Council of Ministers remains the most secretive of the institutions and operates a relationship with TV and the press rather like that of the Kremlin with *Pravda*. Everything is decided in secret and then a bland statement is issued afterwards. The Council is the one institution that should show to Europeans that their governments are really fighting for their interests and only make compromises when that produces a better deal than doing nothing at all. However, it does all of this good work in secret sessions. Is it for fear that they do not want their electorate to see what job they are doing?

Earlier this year, electronic eavesdropping devices were found in the Council of Ministers building. The Greek Foreign Minister, in a breathtaking defiance of the truth, that would not have disgraced the Iraqi information minister, said that he could not understand why anybody should place such bugs, as the Council did everything in the open. I wish that were indeed the case.

The EU has given support to the independent *Euronews* channel in an attempt to enable citizens across Europe to learn what is happening politically, economically and culturally across the member states as well as within the institutions. However, the actual audience figures, as opposed to potential viewers, seem to be very small, and this attempt to help European viewers understand European issues seems not to have met with any great success. Various commercial broadcasting companies, including ITN, have tried to run it and subsequently backed out, and whether it could continue in its present form without the backing of the city of Lyon is open to question. In each member state it is recognised that there is a need for an independent broadcasting organisation, with safeguards of editorial neutrality, that adequately covers the EU if the Union is to become an understandable polity to its citizens. House of Commons and House of Lords debates seem to provide an interesting breadth of material for a specialist BBC Parliamentary Channel as do House of Representatives and Senate debates for C-span in the USA, so why not European Parliamentary debates for a European channel? Live broadcasts could only improve the quality of oratory.

Could Internet be the way ahead, or is it only for the few?

A limited but increasing number of people now use the internet to access information about the EU and its institutions. Whilst the present web-sites are easy for those who know their way around the web and also know what they are looking for, there is no doubt they could be made more user-friendly. Future developments may make it easier and more cost effective to put live web-casts of debates and significant events on the EU web-sites. In any event there can be no doubt but that a good web-site is an important and increasingly significant part of the EU institutions' information strategy. For journalists, students and other opinion leaders it will be the major means of gaining information.

For the year 2002, the Parliament's web-site had an average of some 700,000 hits per day, so there is significant interest, but it is worth recalling that this still only represents little more than 0.2 per cent of the EU population.

Seeing is believeing: good in theory but what about the practice?

In excess of 600,000 people visited the European Parliament in 2002. The total visitors budget for 2002 was 10 million euros, which represents a third of the Parliament's information services' budget. A simple piece of arithmetic reveals, therefore, that 33 per cent of the Parliament's information budget is spent on 0.2 per cent of the population. But does the result, the outcome of visits, justify this expenditure? Does seeing lead to believing?

First hand experience of the institutions should be the best way for people to learn about the Parliament and the other institutions, but the quality of the visitors' experience would seem to be very uneven. There has been little systematic review of the outcome from these visits and discussion of how best to structure them to maximise their effect. Much depends on the quality of the spokesman appointed and the impact made by MEPs who meet their visitors. I suspect that many visitors find it a daunting experience and regard the buildings as opulent and expensive, and possibly assume that the subsidy for their travel means that the EU has too much money to waste. The subsidy could even be counterproductive. The visitors' rooms contain expensive audio visual equipment, so it is surprising that a standard power point presentation or video is not automatically used to set the scene for these visits in a professional manner. A dull monologue by a bored spokesperson on the nth visit of the day will not naturally inspire an audience that may easily become cynical and suspicious – even if it is not so on arrival.

In my experience, visitors all want to know how much it all costs and especially why money has to be wasted on buildings in Brussels and Strasbourg. That is almost a guaranteed question. And the answers are not easy.

It costs more that 2 million euros per year just to move Commissioners to Strasbourg for the monthly meetings, while Parliament spends 169 million euros each year to keep on the move – a figure that will rise to 203 million euros when the EU expands in 2004. That will amount to 16 per cent of the Parliament's budget. Needless to say, this is very costly and inefficient, and hardly an answer likely to win over the hearts and minds of visitors.

The Parliament also arranges visits for a number of national VIPs such as MPs and journalists. The number of British MPs and journalists who come on 'all expenses paid' visits and who then form a more positive impression of the EU is, I suspect, very limited. I would be happy to be contradicted but I do not believe anybody has any facts to contradict my fears. Many of them must travel simply to have their worst suspicions confirmed, and in some cases they return to write knocking copy, biting the hand that fed them.

Plentiful pamphlets: good for re-cycling but are they read?

For the most part, when published by the EU institutions, pamphlets seem to be professionally prepared and presented, although I have never seen the outcome of any consumer testing. I fall back on my own experience of how I see them used, for instance in the visitors centre. There is always an abundant supply of literature, but in every language other than English. I presume more are taken in English, possibly as much a reflection of the need for teaching material in what is becoming Europe's lingua fanca as of the reading habits of Anglophone visitors. But what is appreciated by visiting school and college groups may be less useful for the multitude of senior citizens' groups. Perhaps a clearer idea of the hoped for outcome of these visits and the targeted literature prepared for them would lead to more focused publications which offered better value for money.

I know from visiting local information centres and infopoints that they perform a useful role. Local availability and distribution of information is important. There is a need for paper-based information as well as information in electronic format, and local distribution points could be better used to test the market and reflect back to Brussels just what the consumer wants.

It is clear that the circulation of official literature – pamphlets, brochures, documents – is very limited, and so its impact on wider public opinion about the EU can only be minimal. Information in printed form is necessary and has a role, but it cannot form a significant part of the information strategy. Education is also extremely important, and more and more I find that the younger generations are feeling alienated by politics. This may well explain why many know so little about EU politics, and also about politics in general. Education about politics should form an integral part of any child's school studies, so as to teach them what politics entails and to address the growing ignorance that many people have when it comes to political matters. The EU could do more in providing 'school-friendly publications'.

Conclusions – keep it simple and look forwards not backwards!

For any PR strategy to succeed the product or service it is seeking to promote has a) to be professional and b) to meet the needs of the consumers.

In the 1950s, 60s and 70s it was more obvious and clear that peace and prosperity were closely associated with the growth of the European Union.

In the 21st century, when war between European states seems confined to the history books and when differences abound about how or even whether it is up to government action to promote prosperity, there are no undisputed targets, let alone agreed remedies. A great responsibility rests on the European Convention and subsequently on the heads of government in the member states to produce a European Union that relates to the aspirations and values of the bulk of European citizens of today. Bringing the Union closer to the people is what it is about.

Major problems increasingly traverse national frontiers. Environment, trade, terrorism, international crime, people and drug traffickers, power of multi-national corporations to name a few. Whether Europeans are to be lackeys of Americans in a century of American hegemony or partners for peace and prosperity; these are the issues that the EU must address through its communication with the citizen in its information policy.

Above all the member states must assume more responsibility for explaining to their citizens why they think these problems need to be handled at least in part through the European Union. If the EU tries to blow its own trumpet whilst the member states blow raspberries and put the blame onto the EU for unpopular policies, then any PR strategy is doomed. The European Union's communication and information policy needs to be more co-ordinated, both among the institutions and with the constituent member states. It also needs greater consistency and to be more professionally presented.

Symbolic gestures also have their part to play. As an Englishman I am regularly struck by how the most nationalist of leaders on the continent are confident enough to fly the European Flag on public occasions. The French President never gives a TV interview without the Tricolore and the EU flag side by side. The British Prime Minister should have the confidence to do the same. The first time he did it the xenophobic press might make an outcry. Perhaps the second time, too. But the third time it would start to decline, and after a short while Prime Minister, press and people would appreciate that it is possible to be proud of one's own nation and at the same time be proud of its membership of the European Union. We could fly both flags with confidence, as happens in other European capitals.

Much of the problem of the lack of positive appreciation of the European Union is, however, its own fault. Its policies must make sense in themselves without the need to be explained or excused. Europe – especially the Council of Ministers – must be simpler, more open and straightforward in its actions. Instead of complex formulae on qualified majority voting in the Council, for instance, that few people know and even fewer understand, there must be simpler solutions. What is wrong with the double majority formulae i.e. a majority of states and a majority of population? That would be fair to Malta, fair to Germany, and could be understood equally by the citizen on the Clapham or Calabrian omnibus.

Europe must more rigorously fight fraud, waste and inefficiency. The most monumental symbol of waste and inefficiency of the EU is the double seat of the Parliament in Brussels and Strasbourg. Elderly French and German members claim Strasbourg is a symbol of peace and reconciliation in Europe – and so it was for the 20th century. But the symbolism of the 20th century has little resonance for the voters of the 21st century. Now the most commonly known fact about the European Parliament is that it wastes so much money travelling up and down the motorway between Brussels and Strasbourg. It does not symbolise peace any more but rather gross extravagance: 200 million euros p.a. at the last count, and rising. This, I believe, overshadows much of the EU's good work.

I have proposed that the European Parliament building in Strasbourg should become a European University. We have a postdoctoral centre in Florence and a postgraduate college in Bruges, but as yet no undergraduate institution. The MEPs' offices in Strasbourg would make an ideal student residence and the debating chambers could become lecture halls. Strasbourg would get students there all year round instead of MEPs just 12 weeks a year. Those students would come to love Strasbourg, without doubt; they would most likely come to understand Europe better. This would be a better deal in financial, political and educational terms for Strasbourg, France and the rest of Europe. Strasbourg could then be a symbol for the future of Europe, instead of a symbol of the past.

We need imaginative steps like this, not just for their own sake, buit also for the value to be drawn from them in presentational terms. It comes down both to the policy and to its presentation.

The (Non-)coverage of the European Parliament
Olivier Basnée

Introduction
> *'Overall national media, especially French media, especially audio-visual media, aren't interested in Europe, don't know much about it, decree that it bores everybody, and through that they create and describe a vicious circle, as Ionesco used to say.'*
> Olivier Duhamel, MEP, cited in *Libération*,
> 'Insondables européens', 12 September 2000

From treaty to treaty the EP has progressively become a more important actor, worthy of journalistic account. In the institutional history of the EU, the Parliament has grown ever stronger, so much so that in the recent period of crisis for the Institutions it has finally managed to impose itself as a source of information and an actor in the political life of Europe's citizens.

But most studies dealing with the democratic deficit of the EU use the European Parliament as the key symbol of the problem. The Parliament is assumed to sum up all of the legitimisation problems European institutions are going through. Traditionally, in national political systems, Parliament is the depository of sovereignty; it represents the will of the sovereign people. But as far as the EP is concerned, its marginalisation within the political and institutional system of the EU has turned it into an organ that doesn't fit the usual constitutional canons. MEPs (elected by universal suffrage since 1979) were until recently deprived of any decisional power and still have difficulties gaining visibility comparable to their national colleagues.

When dealing with the legitimacy problem of the EU, most studies adopt a legal approach to the issue. The lack of legitimacy of the whole political system in such a view can be seen as a question of constitutional technology: since the real decision-makers (Commissioners and Ministers) aren't elected and accountable to the sovereign people, the democratic deficit can only be reduced by a legal transformation. Some suggest the election of the President of the Commission by all European citizens; others often suggest strengthening the powers of the EP as a step towards democratising the EU. Seen from another intellectual perspective – the neo-functionalist approach – the gradual legitimisation of the EU political system will be the consequence of increasing integration. As the EU gains more and more competences, a transfer of allegiances from the national to the supranational level will occur. It is the so-called 'spill-over' theory, where political legitimacy ensues from the growing powers of the EU.

These two approaches pose many problems, even if both contain part of the truth. Strengthening the powers of the EP (through real political accountability of the Commission, for example) would no doubt contribute to the legitimisation of the EU, and as the EU deals with more and more issues it may well become a daily – though as yet largely unknown – element in the citizens' life. But the mechanisms that lead social actors to consider political institutions legitimate are more complex than these explanations allow. Allegiance to and recognition of political institutions are historical and social constructs. Such social mechanisms cannot be created by the simple change of legal architecture for the EU. Factors related to representation and belief, to the social image of institutions need to be considered; hence the role played by media in the construction of the popular legitimacy of these political institutions.

Studying the case of the European Parliament, you might question the reason for the lack of media interest for a political institution that is supposed to be the most legitimate among those that make up the EU system. Since it doesn't fit with traditional views of the role and function of a Parliament, the EP suffers particularly from a lack of media visibility. As European citizens don't have a direct perception or experience of this distant political system, it is only through mediation – through the media – that they perceive its activities. However the reasons for the lack of interest in the EP among journalists who cover the EU are numerous and diverse and, if they sometimes have a legal origin, they only make sense when viewed in the light of the practical and intellectual constraints on journalistic activity.

Thus, the role of the EP in the decision-making process, as it is different from that of every national parliament, makes common coverage difficult for journalists from different countries; there is no common background at the EU level. Most cognitive landmarks that enable social actors to interpret political reality disappear or are blurred at the EU level: it is Ministers and not MEPs that – until recently – vote European legislation; it is the European Commission – not the European Parliament – that has the exclusive power of initiating legislation; distinctions between 'right' and 'left' wings aren't relevant anymore; etc. Thus, EU correspondents deal with a novel political system, where traditional political mechanisms aren't relevant. In order to explain the lack of visibility of the EP (rather than of legitimacy, since MEPs are in fact elected by universal suffrage) other reasons have to be found to explain the phenomenon.

The EU Press Corps

There is not a press corps dedicated specifically to the European Parliament, as there is in Westminster with its own lobby system. Very few media organisations can afford full-time journalists to cover only the parliamentary news beat in Europe. MEPs and the EP as a whole have to struggle in a highly competitive environment to get media attention. In competition with various other sources – in particular the Commission and the Council of Ministers – Parliament is penalised by its esoteric functions and its not very newsworthy activities as well as by the anonymity of many of its members.

Added to that, the EU is spread out between three institutional capitals – Strasbourg, Luxembourg and Brussels. The Belgian capital is indisputably the dominant institutional town, both from the journalist's point of view and also for the interest groups. That's the reason why it seems more suitable to talk about the Brussels' press corps even when some of them travel to Strasbourg to cover the EP session there. Geographically speaking, the journalistic centre of gravity is in Brussels;

and there, institutionally speaking, the press corps concentrates more on the Council and the Commission than on the Parliament.

Indeed, it is the European Commission that delivers accreditation for journalists to enter all three major institutions of the EU (Council of Ministers, Commission and Parliament). Except for specific, grand parliamentary events, the Parliament does not have its own accreditation system; the Commission's accreditation is sufficient for the Brussels' press corps to open Parliament's doors. Among the 800 journalists that cover the EU only 40 are registered solely at the European Parliament, an arrangement to allow Strasbourg-based journalists and those who don't fit with Commission criteria[1] to have access to the building of the EP. Thus, the following analysis concerns the EU press corps as a whole since it is impossible to differentiate the coverage of the different institutions that are made by the same journalist. In the Belgian capital, the EP is directly in competition with all the other sources of information available to journalists. And, given its position in the institutional system of the EU, it often plays second or even third fiddle in the struggle to attract journalists' attention.

Morphology of the Press Corps

Number of accredited journalists

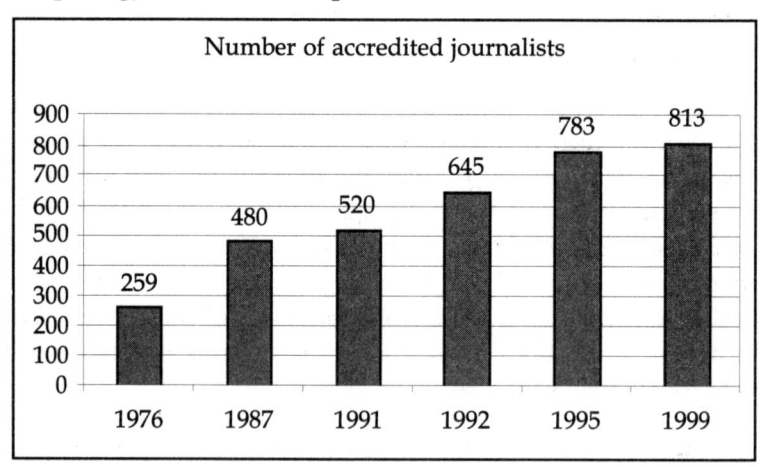

Year	Number
1976	259
1987	480
1991	520
1992	645
1995	783
1999	813

Figure 1: The growth of the press Corps (1976-1999)
Sources: for 1976: Van Hoof G., Essai d'analyse du processus de communication entre la Commission et les agences de presse et autres médias, mémoire, Université de Louvian-la Neuve, département de Communication Sociale, 1978; for 1987-1995: *annuaire des journalistes accrédités auprès de l'Union européenne*, European Commission; for 1999: Gilles Bastin, Les journalistes accrédités auprès des institutions européennes ‡ Bruxelles: groups professionnel, carrières, travail, Mémoire de DEA, Lille 1, Septembre 1999.

As this graph demonstrates, the EU press corps has constantly grown since the beginning of European construction. Within 20 years, it has increased almost fourfold and is now one of the biggest in the world. The Maastricht Treaty and the related growth of the competencies of the European institutions provoked a massive arrival of journalists (125 were newly accredited in one year). Since then there has been a constant growth, and recently Brussels is said to have outmatched Washington as far as the number of journalists is concerned. Depending on which sources one uses, there are now over 800 journalists working in Brussels and regularly accredited to the EU institutions. From enlargement to enlargement their number has grown. National media organisations from Eastern Europe have anticipated their accession (2004) and sent journalists in advance. EU legislation concerning competition, foreign trade and the new competencies in foreign policy probably explain the important groups of US (39) and Japanese (24) journalists. Media from these big countries have realised that more and more decisions that have consequences for their countries, are now taken at the EU level. It is the EU which negotiates the international commercial agreements at the World Trade Organisation, for example.

A major difference with Washington is that there is no advantage for a journalist to be Belgian in Brussels. Unlike the US capital, to be a national isn't an essential asset in information-gathering. According to journalists who have worked in Washington, it is very difficult for a European there to have access to primary sources for information from US institutions. Most of the time these journalists get information through secondary sources. EU correspondents in Brussels, however, aren't foreign correspondents since they have a direct – and not second-hand – contact with sources from their own countries also present there. Journalists themselves often speak of a Brussels posting as 'decentralised' rather than 'foreign'.

Figure 2: number of correspondents by member state. European Commission 1999.

Countries	Number of correspondents	Percentage of the press corps
France	40	7.34 per cent
Great Britain	90	17.06 per cent
Germany	112	20.55 per cent
Spain	47	8.62 per cent
Italy	36	6.61 per cent
Netherlands	32	5.87 per cent
Portugal	13	2.39 per cent
Ireland	7	1.28 per cent
Greece	13	2.39 per cent
Sweden	22	4.04 per cent
Denmark	24	4.40 per cent
Austria	14	2.57 per cent
Luxembourg	6	1.10 per cent
Finland	19	3.49 per cent
Belgium	67	12.29 per cent
Total	545	

Figure 3: number of correspondents by member state, European Commission, 1999.

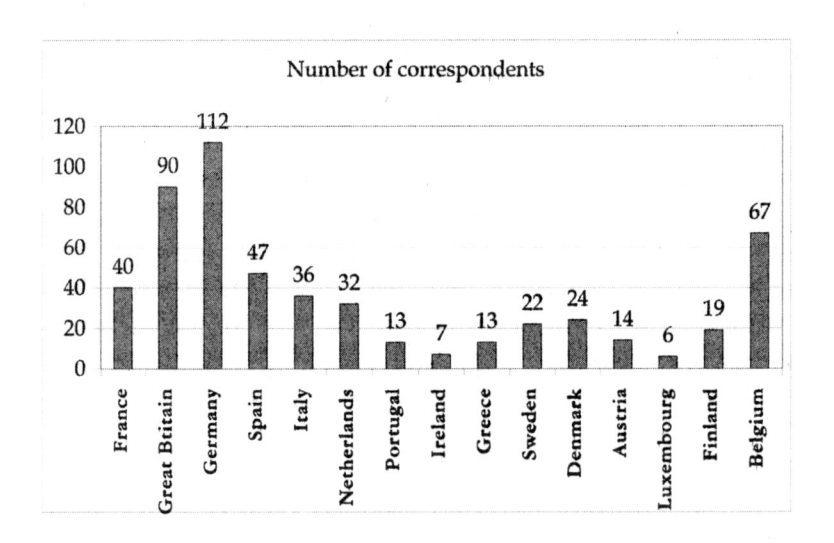

Beyond these questions concerning the accredited journalists themselves, it is useful to look at the organisation of different media to cover the EU news beat. German and British groups represent 40 per cent of the whole journalistic population originating from the member states. The Belgian press is also very important, but that clearly has more to do with geographic proximity than a disproportionate interest for the EU among Belgian viewers, listeners and readers. Apart from these three national groups, no other country represents more than 9 per cent of the press corps in Brussels.

But it can be deceptive to compare the numbers for national groups of journalists since the way they function is not always comparable. There are different professional traditions, national histories and the way each national press organises itself. That's why this article concentrates on a comparison between just two national groups of journalists: French and British. The differences this comparison throws up enable the analysis to avoid taking for granted what are often national peculiarities, and also allows the reader to draw more general conclusions.

French journalists: from expert reporting to investigative journalism

A minor presence

France, as far as the number of journalists is concerned, comes behind Germany, Britain and Spain, and just ahead of Italy and the Netherlands. For one of the founding states of the Common Market, the second largest demographically and an influential member of the contemporary European Union, this low number is surprising. This minor presence is even more striking when one considers that a quarter of all French journalists in Brussels belong to Agence France Presse. While almost all the German and British national medias are represented (except the tabloid press[2]), most French titles are totally absent from Brussels. In the weekly press, *Le Nouvel Observateur* is the only newspaper which has a correspondent, while the national dailies, *La Croix* and *Aujourd'hui* do not have permanent correspondents. In the same way, where some countries – Spain and Germany in particular where the regional political level is relatively powerful – have many correspondents for the regional press, France has very few – only *Ouest-*

France, Dernières Nouvelles d'Alsace, Télégramme de Brest. Even more surprising, the French audio-visual media are almost absent from Brussels: only one television channel (*France 3*) is physically present and only one radio (*Radio France*) has permanent correspondents.

This thin representation can be explained by various factors. The first is geographic proximity, since Brussels is less than one and a half hours from Paris by high-speed train. This encourages the different media organisations to send a special correspondent from time to time, rather than to invest in the opening of a 'foreign' office in Brussels. The uncertain economic health of the French press means that the cost of a permanent correspondent appears too high when compared to their other needs. But there are more fundamental reasons perhaps, since *TF1*, first television channel in Europe, could well afford a correspondent. Europe simply isn't an editorial priority for many French editorial chiefs. This disinterest has to do with the French traditional coverage of the EU which has long been – as we shall see – dominated by a technical approach, offering expert reporting rather than investigative journalism.

Indeed, the French community of journalists is organised around two ideal-types of journalism[3]. These types serve as professional models which allow individuals to personally define their journalistic approach. In fact, these ideal-types relate back to an internal definition process whereby each group justifies to the other its own professional practices.

On the one hand, institutional coverage is characterised by a rather technical and expert-like approach to the EU. Representatives of this model tend to support both the political project of European integration and the specific institutions of the EU. On the other hand, a new kind of journalism has recently appeared which combines investigative reporting methods with a rather critical approach to EU news[4], looking behind the scenes at the political game taking place in Brussels. Representatives of this model legitimate their approach by criticising the journalistic stance of colleagues who have been longer in Brussls. They introduce practices closer to domestic or national political journalism: for example, interest in what goes on behind the scenes, exclusive stories and scandals.

Institutional Journalism

> 'I realised in fact that these people who were here for 30-40 years, who have been here since the beginning, were European campaigners. That is to say, they believed in the European idea. They have made Europe as much as the eurocrats themselves. The have popularised the European idea, they have covered it from the beginning. It's their baby.'

> 'These people aren't journalists in the original sense of the word. That is to say, they didn't see things in a competitive way and they used to see things as a family where everybody takes part in the construction of an ideal.'

For institutional journalists their main role is perceived as that of a 'clerk' documenting EU activities and giving a technocratic or expert daily account of current affairs while providing only a minimum of political interpretation.

Technocratic coverage of EU news de-politicises the nature of the events, the power struggles and the interests which surround them. The conflicts between the various actors (senior civil servants, politicians, lobbyists) never appear; indeed, the only struggles represented are those which oppose member states, as in any traditional form of intergovernmental bargaining. Broadly speaking, these journalists support the official position of the European Commission and are sometimes accused of merely copying the press release they are given at the midday briefing.

As far as their personal profile is concerned, these journalists are also often the veterans of the press corps and are seen as experts on European matters. Five French journalists have been in Brussels for more than fifteen years, and long years spent working with these institutions and the priceless contacts obtained in the time while they were junior journalists rubbing shoulders with the future top officials has transformed them into the 'best address books in Brussels'. Indeed, when evoking a veteran French journalist, one junior journalist simply said, 'This guy is an institution'.

> 'The problem is that, very often, the journalists 'think the right way' because their desire is to be integrated into the machine instead of scrutinising it, criticising it, analysing it, dissecting it. Their dream is to be accepted by those people.'

When they arrived as young journalists (it was often their first assignment) they met people of the same age who were at that time Commission trainees and who later went on to become directors general, senior members of cabinets or even Commissioners. These kinds of acquaintances imply comradeship and friendship with people whom they – as journalists – might otherwise be expected to be able to criticise. Undoubtedly, this relational capital that they have cultivated makes their work easier[5] and is reinforced and legitimised by their 'faith' in the European political ideal. In the past, as long as the press corps was small enough for everybody to know each other, the daily exchanges between journalists and civil servants (especially spokesmen) were very friendly. Not only do these journalists feel that they are part of the European institutional structure but they act as such. The polemics that led to the Santer Commission's resignation are very revealing; while some of their peers were investigating these scandals, other journalists remained silent for as long as they could and, when obliged to write about it, were very sceptical about the accusations and the scandalous nature of the facts[6].

Rather than insisting on what is in fact a relatively 'natural' collaboration between journalists and their sources, as we have seen, more benefit can be drawn from an analysis of this phenomenon in terms of the shared assumptions and beliefs which exist between the journalists and their institutional sources. Since these journalists have both a social and intellectual identification with their sources' world, they have developed a 'reaction of protection of the institution', a kind of self-censorship which they justify by their belief that the Commission is acting for the public good, even if there are occasional lapses of personal behaviour.

Given their support for the European political ideal, these journalists are not very keen to give important coverage to the European Parliament. The Parliament represents for them a place where national and political struggles prevail that tarnish the ideal image of the EU as a shared project for the common European good. Having arrived twenty years ago or more, they grew used to a powerless Parliament, and they were very disturbed when those they consider as petty-minded politicians contributed – by establishing a Committee of Wise Men to inquire about fraud and mismanagement and by publicising whistle-blowing information given by a European civil servant (Paul Van Buytenen) – to throw the Santer Commission out of office.

Investigative reporting and the politicisation of the EU in the media

The 'new species' of journalist constitutes those who define themselves as 'investigative reporters'. They were able to dig out scandals such as those concerning Edith Cresson and other Commissioners as well as the BSE crisis. Unlike most of their peers they do not consider that EU coverage should be limited to experts, and they refuse to hide behind a specialisation which they see as synonymous with a technical, expert-like and hence biased treatment. As they strike a new journalistic pose in Brussels, investigative reporters from France accuse their predecessors of being too closely associated with the institutional actors responsible for the issues that they cover. This new model of journalism highlights their self-definition of a journalist's 'objectivity', demonstrated by their willingness to reveal scandals and dig out scoops. They have decided to treat the EU as they would any other political system, by giving an account of the internal conflicts and struggles that exist within the institutions.

These journalists differ form the institutional journalists due in part to their later arrival in Brussels, largely following the Maastricht Treaty when EU competencies were enlarged and the institutions deeply reformed, the majority voting system extended and the powers of Parliament strengthened. Many have been in Brussels now about ten years. They didn't come to Brussels on the strength of their own conviction or faith in the EU's political project, but they also made the most of their socialisation process within the system. Once their initial learning period was over, their intimate knowledge of the functioning of Europe's political system has enabled them to go beyond the traditional account of decision-taking in Brussels. Indeed, after a few years in Brussels, they have developed their own information networks with which they entertain trusting relationships. They are in a position to understand fully what is at stake and identify the struggles for advantage that fuel their investigative and political news stories.

The investigative reporters' professional methods also differ from those of the institutional ones. The latter have also developed useful contacts inside the institutions and have reliable sources which they protect. However, they do not have the kind of 'reaction of protection of the institution' that is characteristic of the institutional journalists and do not hesitate in revealing compromising information. Moreover, in a journalistic circle which has long been characterised by friendly and intimate contacts, they have professionalised their relationships with sources by, for instance, refusing to dine with officials, or to develop the traditional comradeship which previously existed:

> 'We aren't friends with these people. We are from different social backgrounds. We'll never belong to their social world: we'll never earn as much money as they do, we'll never be civil servants. So, we should never forget what we are: little ....[laughs]'

After arriving in Brussels, which is not itself a very highly regarded position in terms of professional status, these journalists wanted to redefine the traditional EU correspondent's job in a way that conforms more to their professional expectations. In order to do so, they developed practices which are closer to the professional definition of investigative reporting and political journalism. Hence, they tend to be more critical towards the functioning of the EU. Their intermediary position ('europhile' yet critical) makes them a privileged beneficiary of any potential leaks and whistle-blowing. Since they have gained the reputation of being 'investigative journalists', those who want certain documents and facts to become public go directly to them.

They also tend to analyse EU events in a political way, explaining and describing politically the internal struggles and conflicts that take place inside the institution. They consider the EU neither as a technical subject, nor as a wide brotherhood. To them it is a 'continual struggle' between member states, officials, Commissioners, lobby groups and institutions, and they want to give an account of this political reality. In order to do so, they develop a political journalistic style, portraying euro-politicians and writing chronicles of the daily political life of the Union[7] in order to explain what goes on beyond and behind the official discourse.

The combination of these professional methods in daily coverage of the EU turns the 'Brussels post' into a potentially more prestigious and more interesting job for other journalists as well. Even if this new form of coverage is still not widespread in the French press[8], competition between national broadsheets and the retirement of most of the 'institutional journalists' may lead to an increase in the value of EU news since the perception of legitimate ways of reporting Europe is changing. Indeed, this symbolic struggle in Brussels is a reproduction of that which is taking place in the French journalistic field domestically:

the institutional journalists now represent an oddity in a field dominated (since the 80's) by a definition of journalism that tends to privilege exclusives and spectacular news.

The inclination of these journalists for investigative reporting, including the uncovering of scandals, implies among them a very different attitude towards the EP from those of their elders. During the different political and journalistic crises the EU has been through the Parliament has been a first-rate actor and source of information. The EP played a major role in publicising the disclosures of Paul Van Buytenen and put Commissioners in the hot seat by summoning them in front of the Budgetary Control Committee. Finally, by threatening the Commission with a censure motion, it forced it to resign. In doing so, it asserted its role of political control. As the EP grows stronger politically, journalists have been motivated to pay more attention to it, as it tends to produce news stories closer to those in national politics. Indeed, in the inter-institutional balance of power Parliament has become an institution that cannot be ignored by those who wish to give an account of the struggles and of the political tensions between and inside the various European institutions.

British newspapers: EU news through Westminster's eyes

A comparison of French and British journalistic presence among the Brussels press corps shows up significant differences between their level of representation.

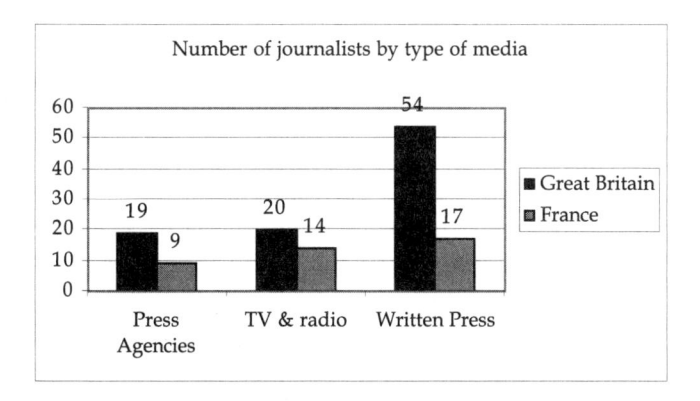

Number of journalists by type of media	Great Britain	France
Press Agencies	19	9
TV & radio	20	14
Written Press	54	17

Three times more numerous in the written press, twice as numerous in the press agencies and with one third more journalists in the audio-visual media: in each segment, British journalists out-number French. And as far as the kind of media these journalists are working for is concerned, the relative weight of the written press is much more important in the British case than in the French one.

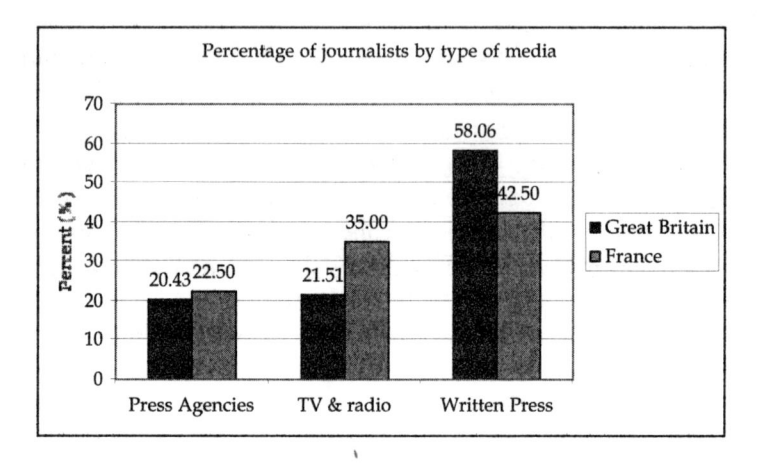

Percentage of journalists by type of media

Media	Great Britain	France
Press Agencies	20.43	22.50
TV & radio	21.51	35.00
Written Press	58.06	42.50

Quite paradoxically, French audio-visual media represent proportionally a bigger part of the French media presence in Brussels. This is the result of a 'zoom effect' due to the number of journalists working for Radio-France (5). But all these journalists, except one, are stringers – as is the one who works for Europe 1. On the other hand, there is an accredited journalists for France 2, but he is in fact Paris-based and only spends two days a week in Brussels.

Similar conclusions can be drawn concerning press agencies: given the small size of the group, AFP is dominant, followed by the other press agency that employs French journalists (Agra Europe) which specialises in agricultural issues.

In the case of the audio-visual media≠ – where the French are under-represented – the British are very strongly present especially with the BBC (17 journalists) and also ITN (2). Reuters is also the press agency which has the largest number of staff in Brussels. Finally, among the written press, one should not overlook the case of the—Financial Times which has an office with 6 journalists, coping with the requirements of the British and the European editions of the FT. Various journalists suggest, indeed, that, in its European version, it is hardly 'a British newspaper at all.

EU as a domestic issue

One of the main differences between the British and French national press is the degree of politicisation of newspapers. While British newspapers clearly have a political line, French ones, using a 'rhetoric of objectivity', refuse to be easily assimilated into an opinionated press. Even where newspapers are politically biased in France, there is no clear editorial stand towards one political party or another. Thus, the political consensus among parties on Europe continues to be reinforced by that of newspapers which, broadly speaking, are all europhile[9]. Even the right-wing *Figaro* has taken a neutral position on Europe since 1992 and the Maasricht referendum.

On the other hand, the British press is clearly divided over Europe[10]. A politicisation of news is therefore possible for them through a domestic political framework. As newspapers confirm and reproduce the clear division that exists in the national political arena, EU news is translated into the national debate. While French coverage is characterised by two rival conceptions of the EU correspondent's job[11], British coverage of the EU can be depicted as being led by a particular newspaper's position on this topic. While working for euro-sceptic newspapers, there is evidence that some journalists were replaced because they were said to show too much leniency towards Europe[12].

Since the 'Maastricht referendum', the EU is no longer the determining factor of French politics. Indeed, among various government parties – Socialst, Gaullist (RPR) and Centrist (UDF) – there exists a widely shared consensus concerning Europe and polemics between national politicians hardly exist on the subject. In Great Britain on the other hand, EU issues are deeply embedded in national politics and some of the fiercest struggles between political parties concern European matters[13]. The only British journalist in Brussels for 15 years explains how his relationships with the editorial offices have evolved over time: 'It was quite an easy job because, as an EU correspondent, I was quite important but there wasn't much to do[14] because the news desk did not want much. But when Mrs Thatcher arrived asking 'what is going on in Brussels? We are losing sovereignty, etc.' then it began and then it became domestic politics. Little by little I've been in continuous contact with my political editor in Westminster. At the beginning there was nothing, it was pointless: nothing to discuss. But with Thatcher: there's something happening in Westminster, obviously there is something here. Each political story is a mix between European and British politics'. After Mrs Thatcher's Premiership turned the EU into domestic politics, it not only became part of the political debate but also part of the national press' political positioning.

This 'nationalisation' of EU news has affected the way in which the group of British journalists organises itself. While the French press corps has two poles of attraction related to two forms of journalism, the British one has only one: Geoffrey Meade, the Press Association's correspondent in Brussels. When asked to name the most influential newspaper among British journalists, every interviewee spontaneously cited this representative of the British national agency, the *Press Association*. He is indeed the key journalist who determines the 'newsworthiness' of any event. As one of his colleagues says 'when he decides it's a story, it's a story' and he himself ironically explains that British journalists consider him as an 'oracle'; his views and advice are certainly listened to with great respect. This influence has three origins. It relates back to his seniority: in Brussels for over fifteen years[15] he is one of very few who has an in-depth personal experience as well as knowledge of the European institutional system. Secondly, each journalist has to bear in mind that Meade's press releases 'are on [their] editor's desk'. Every newspaper subscribes to the *Press Association's* service. The last component of his influence (and the most revealing one) is the fact that his media only covers British current affairs. Given that his entire coverage of EU news is UK-centred, it perfectly corresponds to what the London editorial offices are waiting for.

The 'national filter' which the *Press Association* and specifically this journalist represents is symptomatic of the way in which British newspapers deal with EU news. This politicisation of news is a result of interpretations made in a domestic political framework: is a decision of the Commission likely to embarrass the government or not? As euro-scepticism fuels most of the articles that are written on the EU, corruption and wastage are taken for granted, and euro-scandals are commonplace in British coverage concerning Europe. Paradoxically, since British newspapers and journalists have always considered EU news to be domestic news, they were unable to detect in advance the existence of a real and specific political crisis inside the EU Institutions. Despite having the strongest 'euro-sceptic' press, British journalists did not anticipate the political crisis that lead to the resignation of the entire Santer Commission.

This national perspective has been apparent from the earliest coverage of the UK's relationship with the EU. In 1973, Great Britain – after two unsuccessful attempts – joined the European Community. In 1979 came the first direct elections for the European Parliament. Until that point, delegations from national Parliaments represented European citizens. At that stage the British media tried to export to the European level their strong tradition of parliamentary journalism, but they soon perceived that a Westminster-like coverage was pointless. The example of the *Press Association* is especially revealing.

Within *PA* – as Geoffrey Meade explains it – people asked: 'does this mean that it will be exactly like Westminster?' Does the European Parliament deserve a coverage as extensive as the one applied to the British Parliament? In this uncertain situation, *PA* sent four journalists and put them in charge of writing articles about each British MEP at any parliamentary session. As British MEP's were not elected on a national list but had a local constituency, the idea was to sell such articles to each of the 140 titles of the regional press who, *PA* supposed, would be interested in articles about 'their' MEP. It soon became clear that this strategy was a failure since regional newspapers seemed still much more interested in their MP in Westminster. So the *Press Association* decided to 'repatriate' three of the four journalists it initially sent to Brussels. Nowadays, Geoffrey Meade, while representing a press agency that diffuses its wire news to the entire British press, confesses he only occasionally pays a visit to the European Parliament, and certainly not to every monthly session in Strasbourg.

Given the extreme nationalisation of the interpretation of European political life, the coverage of the EP by the British press appears very under-developed. As the *Press Association* example reveals, after the enthusiasm of the beginning, journalists soon realised that coverage similar to the one of Westminster was impossible and, in any case, didn't interest newspapers much. In a context where the British Parliament is still seen as central, the European Parliament is relegated to the background.

The three different kinds of journalism observed in Brussels can be summed up as follows:

	France	Great Britain
National differences	Long stay	Turn-over policy/rotation
	A group divided between 'institutional' and 'investigative' journalists	Prominent position of Geoffrey Meade
	Weak influence of the Editorial offices	Strong link with London (especially political editors)
	Broadly speaking Europhiles	Eurosceptic basis
Three attitudes towards politicisation	Institutional journalism	Politicisation through national politics (Great Britain)
	Older, in Brussels for more than 15 years	4 or 5 years in Brussels
	Self-assimilation to the institution	Professionalisation of the journalist-sources relationship
	Intellectual and political project	Editorial project ('Prodi killers' for example)
	Investigative/political journalism	
	Younger, arrived in the 90s	
	Distance and reliable sources	
	Professional project	
	Scandalisation	Scandalisation through national politics
Attitudes towards the European Parliament	Disdain for an Assembly of 'minor figures' where national interests are represented and not those of the European Union	Interest for an Assemble which, in crisis times, appears to be an important informer and actor
		Weak interest for a Parliament still less important that Westminster in the Editorial offices' eyes

The French press corps is divided over a definition of what might be the good way of being an EU correspondent and this has strong consequences on the way they cover the EU Parliament. British journalists' attitudes towards the EP are influenced rather by the weight of domestic politics on their coverage of the EU. In both cases, the place of the EP in EU current affairs remains quite marginal. It stems also from the attitudes of journalists themselves abut an institution which has from the beginning of the European project been a minor actor in the EU political game and, as we will now see, with the kind of political life that is lived out in the European Parliament.

A Parliament marginalised by the media?

The rank of the Parliament in the hierarchy of information sources

A highly competitive environment.

In order to understand the place the EP occupies in the hierarchy of sources that feed Brussels journalists it is useful to recount an event that took place on 10 November 1999.

On that day – quite unusually – numerous journalists gathered in the press room of the Paul-Henri Spaak building, which is part of the EP in Brussels. The French Commissioner Michel Barnier and the President of the Commission Romano Prodi had come to explain to the MEPs what the Commission's propositions were for the meeting of Heads of Government due to take place in a few days time in Helsinki. The issue was important since it concerned the way the EU planned to adapt its functioning to the arrival of new members as it enlarged to Eastern Europe. Twenty or so journalists were in the vast press room of the EP, watching the debates which were relayed on a giant screen. A press conference was announced and, as the Commissioner and the President (whose presence wasn't foreseen) were announced, the room soon filled up with other journalists who had come across from the Commission building. The representatives from the national press of the member states then settled down to listen to the Commission's propositions about a crucial issue for the EU's future.

After the Commissioner and the President had finished speaking Giorgio Napolitano, the experienced President of the Parliamentary

Commission for institutional issues, began his presentation, and at that point most journalists left the room.

This attitude is very revealing. The press has little interest for the EP's position even when major issues are at stake. It provoked a humorous reaction from Giorgio Napolitano, who seemed to understand well that the institution he belongs to does not arose enthusiasm among the EU correspondents. Faced with this exodus, he simply 'greeted' (in French) 'all the heroes who have decided to stay'.

One can see in this event the hierarchy between the Commission and the Parliament that exists in the journalists' minds. While the opinion of the former is highly valued and even leads to an unusual number of journalists coming to the Parliament's building when the Commission is there, the latter, even when the journalists are on the premises, cannot hold the attention of the press corps. Even over the enlargement process where the European Parliament holds the power to veto on approving the final agreements, the press does not seem greatly interested by the MEPs' opinion.

While at the national level there is no question about covering the national parliament, at the EU level, such coverage is far from assumed. Indeed, in the political system of information within the EU, the Parliament is not in a position of strength. It has to take into account the other sources of information that, most of the time, appear more immediately useful to journalists.

The European Commission has managed extremely well to establish and maintain prominence in the production of EU news. The institution of a daily briefing that is very well attended (almost one out of three EU correspondents gather every day at noon in the Commission press room) enabled the Commission to have a 'captive public', as a French journalist puts it, from the very earliest years. By circulating its information through numerous press conferences and extensive documentation given to the journalists, the European Commission makes sure it controls the news agenda. As many of the journalists are often responsible for coverage of the entire range of EU current affairs, they have to 'go with the current' of information. Moreover, the Commission personifies more than any other institution the European project. It is the symbol of European integration and the journalists that are supporters of this political project seem to be part of this institution rather than any other – such as the Council, the Court of Justice or even the EP. Some of them – those who arrived as the EU was still in its infancy – are looked on almost as spokespersons of the Commission. One of them (French) has been dubbed the '21st commissioner' by his colleagues as he has very largely adopted the discourse of the institution.

The Parliament, on the other hand, has also to compete with the Council of Ministers which is the next most favoured source of the journalists. Indeed, it is to the Council that journalists come to record the national government's reactions to issues at stake. There is within the Justus Lipsius building (the seat of the Council of Ministers) a large, dedicated press room where members of the Commission and representatives of the Council Presidency come to present the issues and justify decisions taken. But the smaller, national press rooms in the basement of the building still remain the most frequented rooms. There journalists can meet ministers and record the official position of their government concerning the almost daily ministerial meetings. Contrary to what happens at the national level, ministers do not have a monopoly of information at EU level since fourteen other ministers can present alternative versions which contradict what they have just said. Nonetheless, ministers' words are still much more attended to than those of Parliamentarians. Even if, since the Maastricht and Amsterdam treaties, the opinion of Parliament is more and more necessary as the EP becomes a co-legislator, the Council of Ministers still votes European legislation. The opinion of a minister is privileged by journalists over the views of MEPs since the public recognises the former but not the latter. The structural problem for the EP is that, even if its powers have been strengthened since the beginning of the 90s, it is still marginalised in the political and institutional game of the EU. The EP was long considered a totally insignificant actor, a kind 'political dwarf' and still suffers from this institutional image from the past when its legislative role was still minor. As a consequence there is a low recognition factor for most MEPs, and this, in addition to the quite esoteric nature of the functioning of the institution, are also factors that militate against a revaluation of the EP in journalists' minds.

The low media profile of the EP

Figure 5: *Press Presence (average per year)*, Direction de la Presse, DG III, EP, 1995.

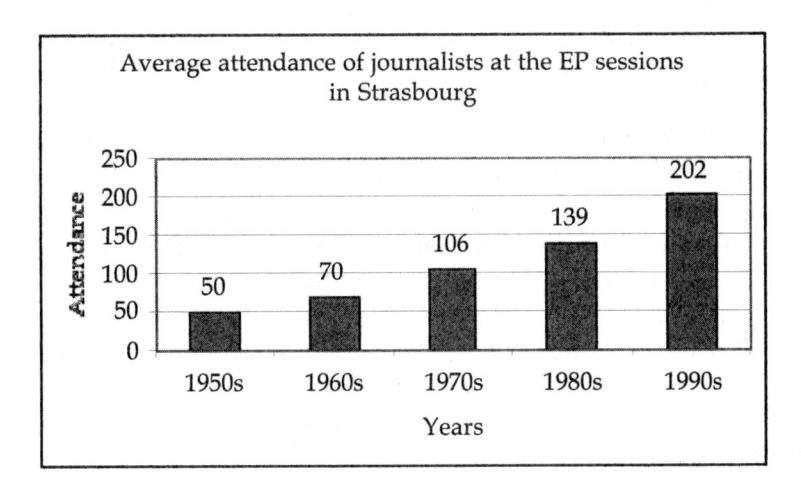

Average attendance of journalists at the EP sessions in Strasbourg

Years	Attendance
1950s	50
1960s	70
1970s	106
1980s	139
1990s	202

These figures seem to indicate a rising interest among journalists for the EP. But they have to be put into context. Even if as many as 200 journalists on average attend the three or four day plenary session of the EP each month, this figure represents only a quarter of the whole accredited press corps. Moreover, 200 is the number of journalists that attend the briefing of the Commission everyday. Furthermore, as the press corps has grown, this rising number of journalists attending the plenary sessions of the EP has remained almost constant as a proportion. Lastly, this figure remains a poor reflection of real newsworthiness as the EP developed for a while an invitation policy towards journalists by reimbursing them their travelling and accommodation expenses. In a context where there is no financial cost for journalists and their newspaper, the fact that only a quarter of the press corps come to Strasbourg once a month is indicative of their low interest in European parliamentary life. Coverage in the press reflects this. In 1999, for example, there were twice as many articles published in *Le Monde* about the Commission as about the EP.

Explanations for the disinterest

Some factors relating back to the functioning of the Parliament contribute to diminish the newsworthiness of the political activities that take place within it. The nature of political recruitment and the quality of MEPs, the language constraints of a multinational assembly and the way the debates unfold and votes are timed are problems that make it difficult for journalists to describe what is happening in the Parliament. Indeed none of these factors fit with usual media criteria of newsworthiness.

'Not a real Parliament' (Mrs Thatcher)

From treaty to treaty (especially those of Maastricht and Amsterdam), the Parliament has become more and more powerful. From a purely consultative assembly, the EP has grown to become recognised as a co-legislative power; through the co-decision process the Council of Ministers cannot decide, without consulting and negotiating with the European Parliament as a partner.

This legislative power, extended by the Amsterdam and Nice treaties and (potentially) the draft Constitutional Treaty, remains limited to the main areas of traditional EP activity. Sectors such as the Foreign Common Security Policy and some areas of co-operation in Justice and Home Affairs remain outside its remit. The second limitation on the role of the EP is that it does not have the right to initiate legislation since that remains a prerogative of the Commission. Finally, although the Parliament exercises a traditional right of Assemblies in parliamentary regimes - that of investing the executive - this right is limited. When the EP invests the Commission, it invests the college of Commissioners as a whole and cannot refuse its support to a specific candidate. The EP sets up individual hearings and sometimes publicises its disapproval about the choices made by national governments (that was the case for Edith Cresson in 1995) but the nomination proceeds nonetheless.

Moreover, even if the Parliament can table a censure motion against the European Commission as a whole, it is very difficult to adopt such a motion – the vote must be by an absolute majority of MEPs and by two-thirds of the valid votes cast. And the EP has no such power vis-à=-vis the Council of Ministers. In the daily functioning of the EU there is no equivalent to a 'governmental majority'. That contributes to blur the balance of power both in the Parliament (where there is no 'government' to cement political coalitions) and between the institutions.

Blurring the interpretative frameworks of parliamentary life

When you look at the daily detail of parliamentary work, it soon becomes clear why journalists have difficulty in reporting it. The constraints implied by multiculturalism and multilingualism pose real problems for European parliamentary life and reporting.

In attempting to address an audience that gathers fifteen nationalities and eleven official languages – and soon to be yet more – MEPs find it difficult to use traditional tools of political communication. Thus humour, for instance, is practically impossible as most of the time it has a purely national resonance. Moreover, references to national historical or cultural backgrounds cannot be easily used, since most of the audience won't understand them. These factors contribute to turn parliamentary debates into a series of dull and often technical monologues, where there is no rhetoric and little lyricism. From the journalistic point of view, debates are not very appealing, and can seldom be used verbatim, which explains why extracts from debates in Strasbourg are rarely used in articles. Political debate is very often absent, since simultaneous translation implies a time-lag between what the speaker is saying and what other MEPs hear in their headphones. Voting is also not 'user friendly' for the general public, as it often consists of a question by the President along the lines of 'Who agrees to adopt the resolution up to paragraph 'x'?'. The opposition seems to consist of conflicts over pieces of phrases, while the issues at stake remain obscure: the detail of the trees obscures the wood. And often the votes are divorced from the debates, sometimes taking place a day or two after the plenary debate.

Another aspect that contributes to diminish the newsworthiness of parliamentary life is the extreme technicality of the issues. The euro-sceptic press has often made fun about technical and obscure dispositions concerning curved bananas or the noise of lawnmowers. But within the Parliament, MEPs often draw their legitimacy from their personal expertise in technical domains rather than from their ability to gather wide political support on more general issues. At the same time, it becomes very difficult and in fact somewhat pointless to try to reduce these debates to more traditional issues of political competition, to arguments between 'left' and 'right'. Journalistic reporting of these debates thus becomes very difficult for the media as they can not make them fit with accepted and well-known forms of political struggle. As one journalist put it: 'Nowadays, I think that in France like anywhere else no one is interested in the balance of power within the EP, who are the leaders of this Parliament, what is said, etc. It may be an institution that has an intense daily activity, but as the EP doesn't lead, for example, a European government and the EP doesn't really control a government of Europe, so what? When we will have a European government, then, I think, most of the political life is going to leave the nation states and will concentrate in Brussels. But not until then.'

As the EP doesn't fit with the traditional political struggle in national terms, it becomes difficult for journalists to give an account of its daily life and role to a national audience. Within the EP, most of the usual interpretative frames for the political game disappear or are, at least, blurred. One of the main obstacles to any coherent account of the political debates that do take place within the EP is the absence of EU political parties and EU-wide campaigns. It is difficult – even if during the election night some programme commentators use these expressions – to differentiate a political majority and a parliamentary opposition.

Indeed, following European elections neither of the two main political groups in Parliament – the European Peoples Party and the Party of European Socialists – have controlled a majority of seats, and so they used often to negotiating before voting, often in concert. It is quite difficult to distinguish a 'left' wing and a 'right' wing in Parliament as a whole, and at the same time, behind the apparent unity of each political group, there are huge ideological variations. To be a liberal in Northern Europe doesn't mean the same thing in Southern Europe (especially in the moral domain); a French socialist following Jospin cannot be likened to a member of Tony Blair's New Labour; and the European Peoples' Party gathers in one Group both the French federalists from the Union pour la Démocratie Française (UDF) and the largely euro-sceptic British Tories.

Most of the time, majorities and oppositions emerge case by case, subject by subject, vote by vote, on bases that are not ideological. Sometimes it will be representatives from small countries versus those from big coalitions, agricultural countries versus industrial ones, etc. The absence of stable coalitions and the fact that they do not necessarily fit with traditional philosophical or ideological divides produces debates that seem abstruse or obscure for audiences that do not know the political actors and are not used to the logic of their European positions.

Invisible actors and their 'theatre'

One of the main problems for the EP, when it seeks to attract journalists' attention, is the relative anonymity of its political actors. This problem concerns many EU political actors (including some Commissioners) but is even more pronounced with the MEPs. The EP is caught in a vicious circle. With weak powers and a low media profile, a career in the EP does not attract the main national political figures. As a consequence it does not benefit from media attention because most of its members remain unknown to most ordinary Europeans. As a political career can rarely begin in Strasbourg and be continued at the national level (because of its poor publicity), political leaders still privilege national elections over European ones. Most of the better known MEPs are already retired from the national political field (as was the case for Valéry Giscard d'Estaing, the former French President) and they are often at the end of their careers.

In addition, MEPs are often regarded by journalists as 'losers' or even 'incompetents' who do not deserve the attention they are looking for. That is especially true among journalists who arrived in the early years of the European construction and who have been accustomed to a EP that was a political dwarf without real powers. This lively memory of parliamentary impotence tends to provoke condescending reactions towards MEPs who are accused of seeking publicity they don't deserve. According to one somewhat arrogant French journalist 'the MEPs need media coverage, so they run after you. They are, most of the time, third-rate absolute unknowns'.

Political powers have always sought to turn their buildings into symbols of their might, but the modest origins, national jealousies and the lack of emblematic identity[16] for the EU have led to a 'branding' policy that has tended to disguise rather than enhance the political nature of these institutions. For many years, the buildings of the EU institutions could hardly be differentiated from the office blocks they are next to. That is still the case for many of them. For a long time, the EP did not even have its own building. In Strasbourg indeed, it hired the building of the Council of Europe until as recently as 2000 when it inaugurated the new European Parliament building. In Brussels, given the opposition of France to the installation of the EP in Belgium, it had to be called an 'international conference centre' to disguise at least in name the growing use of Brussels by Parliament for committee meetings and mini-sessions. The building was immediately nicknamed by the French media 'Caprice des Dieux' because of its excessive cost (12 billion francs) and its appearance, so like the shape of a package of Camembert cheese with that brand name. Deprived of a building until the end of the 90s, the EP has been unable to compete with national parliaments that any citizen is able to identify at first sight: the gilt and the red velvet of the national Assembly in France, or the two parallel rows of benches in Westminster, or even Big Ben. Image is essential, and the EP is short of positive images.

Fort all these reasons, the European Parliament has had and still has difficulty in establishing itself with the media as a player as serious in the European game as the Commission or the Council of Ministers. It will need further changes in the institutional structure of the EU and also in the professional expectations of the media in Brussels and back home in the editorial offices of newspapers and broadcasting organisations before that changes to any major extent.

Notes

1 To obtain the Commission's accreditation, journalists have to justify they live in Belgium, show their national press card and give an attestation from their media that the coverage of the EU is their main occupation.

2 According to the testimonies, this absence reflects back both to economical reasons and to the kind of coverage that is made, which doesn't require the services of an informed correspondent.

3 Of course, very few journalists exactly correspond to these categories (perhaps 7 for both categories out of the 40 French journalists). These ideal-types must therefore only be used as analytical tools.

4 But, they always recall, they aren't eurosceptic - which differentiates them from many British colleagues.

5. They can also take advantage of this relational capital for other purposes. Thus, one of them told me how he acted as a go-between for the industrial group that owns his newspaper. Indeed he has known some members of Prodi's cabinet 'for twenty years'. The firm wanted Romano Prodi to deliver a speech at a meeting. So he did (a recording was broadcast) and the journalist in question wrote the speech.

6 The written article of one of them has even been rewritten and published unsigned as the newspaper considered the point of view wasn't 'neutral' enough.

7 The best example of this tendency is a regular column published in *Libération* called 'Coulisses' [backstage]. This interest for internal conflict is also symbolised by articles such as those *Libération* published about the 'nationality balance' in the Commission, as Romano Prodi replaced some officials and favoured, said the journalist, the British: 'Chaises muicales à la Commission européenne,' *Libération*, 30th September 1999 and 'God save the Commission européenne,' *Libération*, 29th September 1999.

8 In fact it concerns *Libération*, and *Le nouvel Observateur* (weekly newsmagazine).

9 Even the right wing *Figaro* has a very neutral position over Europe since 1992 and the 'Maastricht referendum'.

10 And dominated by euro scepticism: Jeremy Turnstall, *Newspaper Power*, Clarendon Press, 1996, Chapter 15.

11 The institutional journalists' one is, as they are explicit supporters of the EU, intellectual and political but on an individual basis and the critical journalists' is a professional (career-planning) project.

12 Recently, *The Daily Telegraph* replaced its correspondent by a new one who was nicknamed a 'Prodi killer', a journalist whose instructions are to dig out scandals that could embarrass the new Commission President.

13 See for example Peter J. Anderson and Anthony Weymouth, *Insulting the public. The British Press and the European Union*, Longman, 1999, 230 pp.

14 During the interview he remembered he had never played pinball that much in his life.

15 Indeed, he's the only 'foreign' correspondent of the Press Association and no particular status was made for him when he was sent to Brussels. As the agency does not have a rotation policy for its local correspondents he has never been asked to leave Brussels and return to London.

16 The difficulty of determining what belongs to the common emblematic background of Europe was recently symbolised by the difficulty the EU experienced in choosing which monuments to use as decorative features on the 'euro' notes. Eventually the images were computer generated without specific reference to existing national monuments in order neither to give prominence to one or other member state, nor to offend any national sensibilities.

Media and the European Parliament during the Convention
Lars Hoffmann

Introduction

The European Council meeting in Nice in December 2000 culminated in the signing of the Nice Treaty which was supposed most important to prepare the Union for the forthcoming enlargement. However, the Heads of State and Government were not able to agree on all points, and the outcome was far from satisfactory. So it was decided to launch another IGC due to commence in 2004, dealing with residual items and especially with the role of national parliaments in the European decision-making process and the question of the legal status of the Charter of Fundamental Rights.

One year after Nice, the European Council meeting in Laeken decided to launch a Convention in order to prepare the 2004 IGC. The Convention on the Future of Europe was modelled on the previous Convention on Fundament Rights that had successfully worked under the chairmanship of former German President Roman Herzog and had produced the Charter of Fundamental Rights. The Convention on the Future of Europe consisted of a President and two Vice Presidents (Valéry Giscard d'Estaing, Julio Amato and Jean-Luc Dehaene), a representative from each member state as well as each accession country government, two representatives from each member state parliament and each accession country national parliament, two Commissioners and sixteen MEPs. In addition, every member (apart from the President and the two Vice-Presidents) had an alternate, who were allowed to participate in the Convention's debates, even when the full member was present as well.

This meant that up to 32 MEPs took part in the Convention and crucially they all came from the same institution. There were of course up to 108 national parliamentarians (including alternates), but they came from 27 different countries and even more parliaments, since most countries sent representatives from the different chambers of their respective national parliaments. This institutional cohesion was very important and served the European Parliament well during the Convention.

The Brussels press corps has traditionally focused on the Commission and the Council of Ministers. The European Parliament has often been left behind as far as media attention is concerned. Whether that is because of its media-unfriendliness in terms of location (the EP administration is based in Luxembourg, most plenary sessios are in Strasbourg and Committees meet in Brussels) or simply because the press believes that neither readers nor viewers are interested in what is going on in the European assembly is not the main concern of this chapter. The fact remains that many commentators and indeed many MEPs themselves have complained about the media's ignorance concerning the European Parliament's activities. This, however, was changed by the Convention. The seventeen months of this reform-process carried out in Brussels provided the European Parliament with an excellent platform to step into the limelight of European politics and to be at the forefront of media interest.

Why a Convention?

Reforming the Union's institutions to cope with the eastern enlargement has been on the EU's agenda since the 1996 IGC which culminated in the 1997 signing of the Amsterdam Treaty. But Amsterdam produced left-overs which were carried over to the 2000 IGC, and the Nice Treaty again produced left-overs which were mainly concerned with the composition of the European Commission, the extension of qualified majority voting, the role of national parliaments and the legal status of the Charter of Fundamental Rights. Other issues were added to the reform agenda, such as streamlining the Union's foreign and security policy, the question of a common EU defence system as well as the rule for qualified majority voting. This had been altered at the Nice Treaty, but the outcome was not satisfactory to anyone but Spain and Poland (who benefited disproportionally from the new settlement).

The problem of previous IGCs has been that the member states' governments were caught up in complicated negotiations attempting to achieve a Pareto efficient outcome whereby no member state was worse off than before the negotiations. This led inevitably to last minute compromises, which lacked clarity and added complexity to the Union's *modus operandi* rather than contributing to greater efficiency and transparency. The qualified majority voting rules agreed in Nice are a prime example whereby the outcome makes no member state worse off than the previous rule but it is extremely complicated, involving a three-hurdle majority for any legislation to pass the Council under the qmv-rule (a majority of the weighted votes, a majority of member states and at least 2/3 of the EU's population).

The Convention on the Future of Europe was modelled on the first Convention on Fundamental Rights and it was hoped that this second Convention, working as effectively as the first, would prepare a text that would serve as a basis for the intergovernmental negotiations. Thus it would take some pressure off the governments, as in theory the most contentious issues (such as qmv and the number of Commissioners) would be already resolved by the Convention.

As the Convention was intended not only to function as a preparatory body for the 2004 intergovernmental conference but also to increase its legitimacy, it included not only government representatives but also Commissioners, representatives from the national parliaments and members of the European Parliament. This inclusiveness was a new step in European reform processes. In the preparation of the Maastricht Treaty and the launch of the European Monetary Union, there has never been a similar inclusiveness in the EU reform processes. But for this Convention the member states' governments decided to put their representatives on an equal footing with representatives from other institutions. Moreover, government representatives were only a small majority within the Convention, so it was much harder for them to dictate the agenda in the way they are naturally able to do during an intergovernmental conference.

The special role of the European Parliament

Although the European Parliament only contributed 16 out of the 102 full members it soon become clear that the MEPs taking part in the Convention would play a special role and be able to influence the Convention's work much more effectively than other players. In his maiden speech as President of the Convention, Valéry Giscard d'Estaing called for the drafting of a European Constitution. By this he reinterpreted and enlarged the mandate given to the Convention by the Laeken Summit. Giscard's initiative was greeted with general support and had in addition two specific consequences. First, it stimulated great media interest, as a Convention drafting the first European constitution was potentially more interesting than an IGC-preparation committee. Second, it put the European Parliament in an ideal position, as it was the EP itself that had started the 'constitutional debate' back in the early 1980s when Altiero Spinelli, then an MEP, drafted his European constitution which was adopted by the European Parliament. The European Parliament has been traditionally the intellectual driving force of European integration, but prior to the Convention it had been kept on the sidelines of the EU reform process. The Convention, for the first time, offered the European Parliament a chance to voice its opinion alongside other accredited actors such as national governments and national MPs, and to actively influence if not direct reforms of constitutional importance at the highest European political level.

From an intellectual point of view, the EP was well prepared to be an active participant in the European Convention and put forward strong opinions. The fact that it traditionally is able to act as a cohesive body on the basis of consensus as opposed to national parliaments which are often divided by strict party political lines was clearly beneficial to the EP's position in the Convention. The decision-making process in the Convention was also based on consensus. No votes were taken on the Convention floor, and it was up to the Convention Praesidium to decide where exactly the consensus lay. Without going into the debate whether this was a good method of decision-making, it meant that a cohesive group of Convention members voicing the same opinion were able to influence the debate considerably. Members of the European Parliament met according to party affiliation prior to Convention meetings as well as meeting as a whole, and were thereby able to strengthen their influence in the Convention. Representatives from other institutions, such as national parliaments and national governments, were unable to form an equally cohesive group. National governments have traditionally different opinions and priorities – clearly apparent as it was they who were not able to come up with satisfactory solutions at Amsterdam and Nice. National parliamentarians were in a particularly awkward position; they had never been involved in European treaty reforms before. Although responsible for ratifying new European treaties, they had never had any representatives at previous IGCs. Individual MPs from different nations did not know each other before the Convention, and it was therefore very difficult for them to form a cohesive group. This was reinforced by the fact that national parliamentarians think and act much more on party political grounds than MEPs, making co-operation among them more difficult. Added to that, most parliaments sent one representative from the main government party and one from the main opposition party.

Members of the European Parliament had one other advantage vis-à-vis their national counterparts and the government representatives: they were 'natives'. They live and work in Brussels; they have offices and staff there; and they know how Brussels works. The fact that Convention meetings were held in the European Parliament building reinforced this advantage even further. Representatives from national parliaments mostly had never been to Brussels and did not have any administrative infrastructure to hand. Most of them stayed in hotels and the only way to communicate with other *Conventionels* was during or immediately prior to Convention meetings. Members of the European Parliament on the other hand had their staff on site. They had offices, access to computers, faxes and telephones. They were contactable not only by fellow MEPs but also by the press. A national parliamentarian had to rely on his mobile phone whereas an MEP had his fully equipped office to back him/her up.

The Convention's media appeal

The call for a European Constitution was certainly the trigger for the strong media attention the Convention received right from the beginning. Parallels with the Philadelphia Convention that produced the US Constitution were quickly drawn and provided the press with a story that had an appeal to a wider public throughout the Union. Although the reaction to a European constitution differed from country to country (the German public was much more enthusiastic about the possibility of a European constitution than the UK public which was if anything opposed to the idea) the interest in the press was considerable. Something new and exciting was happening in Brussels.

Previous IGCs were mainly fought out behind closed doors in late night sessions between heads of state and government, supported by their ministers and civil servants. Reporting on what actually happened during these negotiations was based largely on guesswork and more or less reliable inside sources rather than public facts and official commentaries, and never on first hand observation of the negotiations. This was clearly different within the Convention framework. Discussions happened in the open; national governments had to come clean about their positions and their 'red lines', something they could hide or dissemble in the context of media reports on an IGC. The Convention was open to the press, the public, civil society as well as academia; all were encouraged (by the Laeken declaration itself which laid stress on openness and transparency) to participate in the debate. This meant that the media had direct access to the debates as well as to the Convention members. No longer was it necessary to rely on inside sources and second-hand reports. It was now possible to confront Convention members about the ongoing discussions and their personal opinions, and to press them to defend their positions to the media.

The Convention not only stimulated media interest because of its openness; it went on to develop internal dynamics and processes which caused great media interest. The openness of the plenary meetings was countered by the secrecy of the Praesidium meetings. The Convention Praesidium was made up of the President and the two Vice-Presidents, the government representatives of the three countries that held the EU Presidency at the time of the Convention (Spain, Denmark and Greece), two MEPs, two national parliamentarians, two Commissioners, and one representative from the accession countries (the latter only after intense lobbying from the accession country members of the Convention). The Praesidium was supported by a Secretariat, which did most of the drafting work during the Convention's final stages and was headed by the high-ranking British civil servant, Sir John Kerr. This combination of the Praesidium, chaired in a very presidential manner by Giscard d'Estaing and meeting only behind closed doors, and the even less visible Secretariat may have decreased the Convention's openness, but it further enhanced media interest. The combination of openness and secrecy was an ideal recipe to create media attention.

MEPs in the limelight

The European Parliament was in a strong position to benefit in media terms from the Convention and it took full advantage of this situation. The EP had two representatives in the Praesidium, former EP President Klaus Hänsch and Spanish MEP Iñigo Méndez de Vigo. This provided the European Parliament delegation as a whole with valuable inside information as the two MEPs were able to report back to the other MEPs during their caucus meetings prior to Convention plenary sessions. The whole 'institutional group' of MEPs were much better informed and had much more detailed information about ongoing processes in the Praesidium than other groups such as national parliamentarians who did not meet in such a coherent and well-organised form as their European counterparts.

Members of the European Parliament soon emerged as opinion formers and leaders among the Convention members. They were well informed about EU processes in general and had a clear opinion about 'their' vision of a future Europe. Two of the most prominent thinkers among the MEPs – though at opposite ends of the spectrum - were Andrew Duff (UK) and Jens Peter Bonde (DK). These two were regarded as the leaders of the euro-federal and the euro-sceptic camps among Convention members. They often featured in the press and provided for interesting stories, thereby increasing media interest in the Convention and the work of the European Parliament within it. Compared to this, many national parliamentarians appeared to hold much less strong opinions and adopted a more passive approach to the Convention's working process. The media focus was therefore much less on national parliamentarians than it was on MEPs.

Media attention concerning the Convention peaked for special events, such as the launch of the Convention in February 2001, the start of the working groups, the launch of the Franco-German and Spanish-British proposals on institutional reform in January 2003 and the final debates in May and June 2003, which dealt with the big institutional questions. Other events such as Giscard's remarks about

Turkey's unsuitability for EU membership also led to increased media coverage, although perhaps for much less desirable reasons. For all of these events the European Parliament was in a well-prepared position as it had previously formed opinions and discussed issues related to the European Union's future development (including Turkey's EU membership). MEPs are European politicians and were well placed to engage trenchantly in an official reform process which aimed at creating a European constitution. As a result the media increased its interest in the European Parliament in general, and specifically its members' work within the Convention. For the first time MEPs were not dealing with regulations concerning the details of legislative harmonisation of rather obscure items of little media interest; it was an important player in a great European undertaking.

MEPs, even those that were not part of the Convention, engaged in the debate and – with 'Europe' being their job – they all had a well-formulated and thought-through opinion on why and how things should change and in particular be made more efficient and transparent. In addition, they were in a very flexible position compared to other Convention members. National parliamentarians often came to the Convention without a pre-fixed opinion and national government representatives were bound by the instructions given to them by their governments at home. German government representative and foreign minister Joschka Fischer, for obvious reasons, was not able to answer questions and formulate opinions as open and frankly as German MEP and Convention Praesidium member Klaus Hänsch. The combination of strong opinions based on well thought-through arguments, and the possibility to speak to the press with hardly any institutional restrictions, meant that the members of the European Parliament became an ideal focus for the media and received much greater attention than under normal circumstances.

Conclusion

During the seventeen months of the Convention on the Future of Europe the European Parliament played an important role in the Europe-wide media. Its expertise and willingness to co-operate openly with journalists meant that MEPs moved much more into the media limelight than might have been expected. Exposure differed from country to country, but across the continent the profile of MEPs was raised, and with it their Institution. Indeed, Parliament actively sought media attention. One example is a major conference that was organised by the European Parliament Office in the UK part way through the Convention which attracted not only high profile speakers (from within the European Parliament as well as other Convention members and policy makers) but also considerable press attention. Similar events elsewhere also gained local and national press coverage.

Now that the Convention has finished its work, a question remains: will the increased media attention in the EP's activities continue or will it drop back to the pre-Convention level? The answer may well lie somewhere in the middle. The European Parliament benefited from the special circumstances of the Convention. It had the logistical and intellectual capacity to provide an excellent partner for the press during a time of high media interest. Many members of the European Parliament have now made valuable contacts with the press; some indeed have made a European if not an international reputation. Although the media interest in the European Parliament may decrease compared with the time of the Convention, some spill-over is likely to occur and the EP on the whole, and certain individual MEPs specifically, will certainly benefit from greater media attention than they received in the past.

E-Coverage of Europe
Stephen Coleman and Bridie Nathanson

Democracy and European governance

While at the peak of its success in terms of international spread and acceptance, democracy is facing a crisis of confidence in its ability to connect with the experiences and aspirations of ordinary Europeans. At European, national and local levels of governance, there is significant distrust of politicians, declining party allegiances, disappointment with the power of governments, and, unsurprisingly, low voter turnout in almost all elections. While there is still lots of political activism and engagement, it is mainly on a single-issue basis, and often channelled outside traditional governmental institutions. The credibility of national democracies is challenged in a global world, and while supra-national governance is growing, it is perceived as not managing to fill the gaps.

In the wake of debates about the incapacity of national governments to act, reduced autonomy caused by globalisation and policy leakage beyond national boundaries, the democratic credentials of transnational governance are increasingly under the spotlight. The EU is the most developed example of supra-national governance. With an elected assembly, it is also the most democratic. Yet it suffers from a highly visible democratic deficit, bringing with it fundamental legitimacy questions.

The emergence of e-Democracy

e-Government, and to a far lesser extent e-Democracy, have taken root in the thinking of most governments, and are already transforming the way citizens interact with government. While e-government is driving transformation in the overall relationship between governors and citizens, it is doing so on an organisational and operational level, not a democratic one. Although still untested, e-democracy has the capacity to engineer equivalent transformation, albeit more as a catalyst than an all-in-one solution. It is an enabler rather than a solution, but e-democracy brings with it the opportunity and the motivation to tackle democratic deficit and engagement problems.

Early advocates of e-democracy envisaged a substitution of representative institutions by direct, push-button democracy, but such schemes have been largely speculative and shown as politically unrealistic. e-Democracy, as we discuss it in this chapter, is about using new information and communication technologies (ICT) to strengthen representative democracy. The contemporary e-Democracy menu comprises elements of e-voting, e-consultation, e-participation and e-engagement. It can be regarded as all of these things, and more. But most importantly, it is more about the 'democracy' than the 'e'.

e-Democracy is being deployed for various purposes in a wide range of countries: to enhance the legitimacy of government decision-making through mass public consultation exercises (Canada, Denmark, Finland); to improve the quality of legislation through online contact with experts or hard-to-reach groups (Australia, Sweden, UK); to develop party policy (Canada); and to make voting more convenient (Switzerland, South Korea, UK). Broadcasting and webcasting of parliamentary or council sessions occur in many countries (Iceland, France). In several countries representation is being enhanced through online debates, e-polls and increasing email contact between citizens and elected representatives.

Everywhere e-democracy is being experimented with in an ad hoc fashion, with the consequence that nowhere is it really being put to the test. A template for a comprehensive e-democracy strategy, which addresses a range of democratic needs (rather than technical possibilities) is required. It is the challenge of this chapter to develop such a template, which can be applied to European Union institutions.

Key challenges

In developing an e-democracy strategy to address the EU's democratic deficit, there are a number of fundamental issues to be addressed which relate directly to the role, activities and functioning of particular EU institutions, as well as regarding the EU in the multi-layered governance context in which it sits.

The EU has long been criticised for its perceived and real lack of openness and transparency. These criticisms range from the complex division of institutional responsibilities and decision-making processes, to the inner workings of institutions and the extensive use of undisclosed and unaccountable experts, or the basic (un)availability of information pre- and post decisions, and the general inaccessibility of the system to all but a small minority of Europeans citizens.

Participating in European policy or decision-making has traditionally been another 'out of bounds' area for most Europeans. While there are a myriad of European level groupings of local organizations, there is no evaluation of how effective their role is within the policy-making process, especially compared to the more well resourced lobbies, often from the private sector. Guaranteeing opportunities for direct and effective participation to all European citizens and organisations in policies which affect or concern them is a minimum requirement that must frame a strategy for a more democratic Europe. An important corollary to this could be described as enhancing the quality of discourse and understanding. It is not enough to enhance public debate or participation if this lacks substance and has little impact in informing the public.

Another important challenge is effectiveness of governance. Any strategy designed to improve democratic processes must offer an improvement in outcomes. At the same time, these outcomes must be fair in terms of both substance and procedure. Additional important criteria to be considered in the development of an EU e-democracy strategy include representation, control of agenda, and accountability, all of which must be attended to. Finally, there are the challenges that come with all things 'electronic': e-inclusion, ownership and regulation of new democratic tools, technologies and processes, and integration of the online and offline.

Key Opportunities

While the challenges loom large, the prizes could be rewarding enough to merit the effort. Successful innovation and reform of democratic processes at the EU level would bring increased democratic legitimacy, and possibly increased public support and interest. This in turn would make acceptance, compliance and enforcement of EU regulations and laws at the national level more likely, thereby improving the effectiveness of European governance. Internally, inter-institutional relations would become easier, with a related increase in efficacy and efficiency. Internationally, the EU's position would be strengthened, especially given its renewed democratic legitimacy vis-à-vis the other institutions of international governance.

In addition to the democratic rewards there is another more political prize: e-leadership. In all areas of new technology, from technology development to e-business, e-commerce, e-procurement and e-government, there is strong competition for first place. This competitive contagion has infected all governments worldwide. In the race to pioneer best practice, the government sector is inundated with studies and surveys, benchmarking and best practice case studies. All EU member states are grappling with the same problems, including those of democratic legitimacy and engagement. The EU can win the gold medal if it is the first to successfully tackle these issues.

An e-Democracy Strategy for Europe

The key components of an e-democracy strategy are:

- Information: a uni-directional flow of information from governor to governed.
- Communication: a general two-way interaction between governor and governed, ranging from opportunities for open dialogue to government-solicited feedback and response such as consultations
- Participation: opportunities for citizens' democratic participation, not instigated, conditioned or limited by governors
- Representation: the process of one's interests being articulated in policy and decision-making, within both parliament and governing institutions
- Accountability: the requirement for governors to explain and take responsibility for their decisions or actions

- Evaluation: all of the above elements should be underpinned by continuous evaluation and monitoring of both process and impact.

These elements listed above are considered to be integral to developing a complete e-democracy strategy, all of which are intertwined and mutually support each other. Information provides the basis for openness and transparency, informing and enhancing quality of public discourse. Communication is necessary to build the relationship between governors and governed, providing vital links for information flows, which occur through consultation processes. Possibilities for direct and effective participation, as previously discussed, are central to the democratic process, but also provide for fairness and loosening government control of the political agenda. Communication and participation both contribute to enhancing representation, ensuring citizens' interests are represented, whether solicited, volunteered or researched. Both information and communication are central to accountability, on the basis of which citizens can participate by registering their approval/disapproval with the way their interests have been represented. Thus, all of these elements can be seen to contribute to improving the effectiveness and democratic legitimacy of governance.

In addition to the key elements listed above, an e-democracy strategy must embrace an integrated approach to democracy, addressing a variety of processes and activities, using multiple channels. Avoiding social exclusion, or dealing with the digital divide, also requires attention. While ensuring that e-democracy activities are multi-channel, more active inclusion policies will help to ensure that e-democracy strategies are truly democratic. Evaluation of e-democracy activities, which would involve monitoring levels of information penetration and participation among vulnerable groups, is a key part of the strategy.

e-Democracy should not be conceived solely in the context of 'formal' governance. It must cater for various audiences and include different types of democratic actors, from parliament, government and governing agencies to civil society, social partners, private sector representative bodies, and the media and information sector, as well as unorganised protest movements and individual citizens.

Fig. 1 Overview of e-democracy strategy

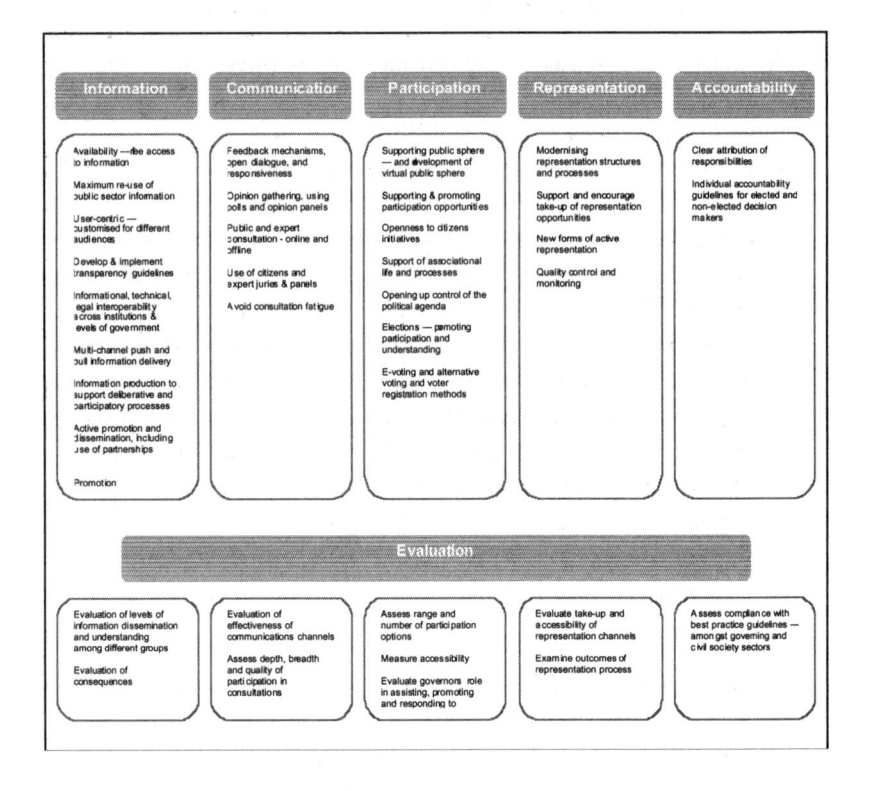

Information	Communication	Participation	Representation	Accountability
Availability — free access to information	Feedback mechanisms, open dialogue, and responsiveness	Supporting public sphere — and development of virtual public sphere	Modernising representation structures and processes	Clear attribution of responsibilities
Maximum re-use of public sector information	Opinion gathering, using polls and opinion panels	Supporting & promoting participation opportunities	Support and encourage take-up of representation opportunities	Individual accountability guidelines for elected and non-elected decision makers
User-centric — customised for different audiences	Public and expert consultation - online and offline	Openness to citizens initiatives	New forms of active representation	
Develop & implement transparency guidelines	Use of citizens and expert juries & panels	Support of associational life and processes	Quality control and monitoring	
Informational, technical, legal interoperability across institutions & levels of government	Avoid consultation fatigue	Opening up control of the political agenda		
Multi-channel push and pull information delivery		Elections — promoting participation and understanding		
Information production to support deliberative and participatory processes		E-voting and alternative voting and voter registration methods		
Active promotion and dissemination, including use of partnerships				
Promotion				

Evaluation

Evaluation of levels of information dissemination and understanding among different groups	Evaluation of effectiveness of communications channels	Assess range and number of participation options	Evaluate take-up and accessibility of representation channels	Assess compliance with best practice guidelines — amongst governing and civil society sectors
Evaluation of consequences	Assess depth, breadth and quality of participation in consultations	Measure accessibility	Examine outcomes of representation process	
		Evaluate governors role in assisting, promoting and responding to		

To be successful, the e-democracy strategy must be integrated vertically, horizontally and politically. Vertical integration means sewing e-democracy practices into the operating of governance institutions and agencies at different levels, from the local up to the national and the European. Horizontal integration entails linkages between different types of institutions (parliaments or assemblies, government ministries, departments and agencies, non-government partners involved in policy development or implementation) and across policy areas. Political integration requires e-democracy practices to connect with the political process, from pre-policy through all aspects of the decision-making cycle to implementation and feedback. Without this type of integration, the incentive for public participation in e-democracy activities and outcomes becomes opaque.

Information strategy

The information strategy needs to address issues of access to and accessibility of all public sector information, including its re-use.

• *Availability of all EU information*

There should be free public access to all public sector information produced by the EU Institutions. This rule should extend, where possible, to any information submitted to the institutions, which inform or influence decision-making. Any exceptions to this rule (for security reasons, for example) should be clearly stated, described and explained.

Re-use of EU information should be maximised, especially via the free and most successful subscription channels. Information should not only be made available in easy to reproduce or re-purpose formats, but there should be active promotion amongst these channels.

• *User centred and accessible*

The provision of information in a user-focused way is key. This means the selection, design and presentation of public information which is customised to meet the needs of the various audiences, whether professional bodies or individual citizens. It means explicitly catering for hard-to-reach or special needs groups, such low income, illiterate, disabled, minority languages etc. User-centricity entails bundling or grouping different pieces of related information regardless of source or author, as happens with the 'life events' type of presentation now common in many national and local e-government services.

• *Transparency*

In tackling the democratic deficit, public confidence in governing institutions will not be restored without new transparency guidelines, including what kind of new information needs to be produced.

• *Inter-operable information presentation and management*

'Inter-operability' should be taken to mean a seamless integration of information from multiple governance sources – regardless of institution type or level – requiring institutions/authorities to be able to locate and handle government information without difficulty. (This implies technical, legal, organisational, cultural and informational inter-operability.) Most EU citizens can neither distinguish between the different competences of their local, national and EU authorities, nor the differing roles of parliament and government departments in policy-making or the implementation process. While these distinctions could be made clear, a one-stop information shop, providing intuitively linked information is necessary. This requires inter-operability for authorities to be able to bundle or package related information.

This inter-operability could be extended to non-government actors (for instance the media, social partners or representative bodies) who have a role to play in the democratic process and sizeable audiences to warrant the effort.

- *Multi-channel 'push and pull' delivery*

The provision of information must be multi-channel: delivered using new technologies (e.g. internet, email, text messaging, interactive TV) where desirable, appropriate and effective, but not to the exclusion of traditional delivery mechanisms, such as print, telephone, face-to-face and through the use of intermediaries such as the media, private, public and non-profit sector organisations.

In addition, the use of 'push and pull' information delivery, greatly enabled by new technologies, should be used to enhance the customisation of information flows. Using a multi-channel delivery system, users can determine what information they actively seek out or 'pull' from the internet, and what information they want to be automatically sent or 'pushed' to them, e.g. via email. In this way, a variety of information delivery mechanisms will allow for optimal and customised delivery to different audiences.

- *Information production*

Information generated during the course of parliamentary or institutional activity, whether draft bills or national statistics, is rarely the stuff of stimulating public interest or energising public debate. Information strategies must now include room for generating new types of information – whether relating to questions of public concern (e.g. new demands for transparency and accountability) or producing appropriate material designed to support educational and deliberative processes. (This new information may take the form of printed material, electronic data, video-audio footage or otherwise.) This said, the fine line between this new democratically required information and that produced for propaganda purposes must be carefully defined and observed.

• *Active news and event-based promotion and dissemination*

Competing for 'eyeballs' in the 'attention economy' is one way of describing the problem of information overload. Any successful information strategy must include a corollary - an active promotional strategy - designed to generate interest in and understanding of issues, and stimulate and support related communication and participation processes. Promotion must be active, including news and events-based strategies, multi-channel promotion (ranging from ads in the broadcast media, to viral email and text messaging (SMS) campaigns), the development of contact strategies and partnerships with intermediaries, particularly with regard to the less informed groups.

• *Evaluation of information dissemination and consequences*

No information strategy is worth its salt without a serious evaluation. In attempting to address the democratic deficit, it is essential to gain an understanding of levels of information dissemination and understanding, how far information is reaching the target audiences, and to what effect (e.g. reducing public fear, concern, or even support for the policy). This insight will assist in the allocation of resources for further information provision.

Communications strategy

Alongside information, communication forms a crucially important strand of this strategy. Communication can be taken to include general two-way interaction between governor and governed, ranging from one-to-one dialogue to government solicited feedback and response such as consultations, citizens' juries or panels, or even opinion-gathering exercises. The objective of this element of the e-democracy strategy is to maximise the range of options decision-makers have to inform policy development and decision-making on the one hand,

and the opportunities for citizens, or representative groups, to feedback on the other.

• *Feedback mechanisms and responsiveness*

There is a need to guarantee existing and create new communications channels for open dialogue between governors and governed. This may range from solicited or unsolicited feedback to governing authorities on policy implementation, to voters' requests for assistance from their parliamentary representatives.

Implicit in this notion is response. Governors have a responsibility to respond to communication from citizens, and in so doing, providing an indication of how their communication will be dealt with and what – if any – further action will be taken. Response is an important part of government communication – without which citizens will soon stop communicating and participating. Quality and time of response therefore all need to be monitored and public expectations met.

• *Opinion gathering*

Opinion or attitude research often provides policy and decision-makers with a general barometer of public thinking. Online polls and opinion panels, both conducted equally effectively using new technologies, can be useful first-base tools for gauging the public mood on specific issues.

• *Public and expert consultation*

Integrated consultation (both online and offline) is a central feature of e-democracy. Consultation of appropriately concerned, involved and experienced parties can take place at any stage in the policy and decision-making cycle. Consultations can be used both as consensus building exercises as well as the more oppositional, discursive ones – depending on the policy area and stage in the policy cycle. Citizens juries or panels, often online, are additional forms of more continuous consultation, and can also be developed as deliberative tools.

Online consultations must comply with generally accepted rules for best practice, including appropriateness of type and method of consultation for target audiences, maximising breadth and depth of participation among target groups, proper management of expectations of consulted groups, and a clear link to results or outcomes in the policy process, with subsequent feedback to participants.

• *Avoid consultation fatigue*

A note of caution should be sounded on the subject of consultation overload, or fatigue. The level and quality of participation in consultations may decrease with increasing frequency. This makes it particularly important that different consulting authorities coordinate, and where possible amalgamate their activities.

Participation strategy

Active participation of citizens in the democratic life of their district, region or country, is a core objective of e-democracy. While governments and governors should not determine or condition this activity, they should play a role of facilitation, stimulation, promotion and support where possible and appropriate.

• *Support for the public sphere*

While the public sphere is protected and well developed in most democracies, as we move into a world where more and more of our social, business and governance activity occurs online, the development of a virtual public sphere becomes increasingly important. Governing institutions must invest in the creation and maintenance of this space - by independent, non-government groups - in which public debate, scrutiny and democratic activity can take place. The establishment of such protected democratic space should be addressed at a European level, involving the co-operation of all national authorities and other democratic actors.

• *Supporting and promoting participation opportunities*

Government assistance to the civil society, voluntary or community media sectors is important in providing opportunities for democratic involvement. Deliberative processes and public debate undertaken by non-government actors should be supported by government through the provision of relevant customised information. Governments are increasingly engaged in sophisticated information management and presentation, based on user-centric research. This competence could be applied to the support of citizens during public debates or in referendum periods – or at least provided to independent actors in the public sphere.

In addition, government should apply resources to promoting participation opportunities in general, given its extensive network of public outposts, its multiplier networks and its access to media, as well as promoting specific issues requiring wider public awareness, understanding or inputs.

Nowadays there is much scope (and demand) for more innovative forms of public engagement, through TV/radio programmes and virtual or social event-based strategies. Government must explore supporting these more innovative approaches.

• *Associational life*

Associational life is central to democratic culture. Governments and institutions can support participation by helping citizens 'associate' - whether getting involved with existing organisations or setting up their own – through directing citizens to alternative groups or options at every sign of disappointment or frustration in areas of policy or interaction with government. Moreover, stimulating or co-ordinating a self-regulatory culture or the instigation of accountability and transparency guidelines among civil society associations will assist in developing public trust and the ability to evaluate alternative options.

• *Public control of the agenda*

Opening up control of the political agenda beyond the political and governing elites is a key democratic criterion. Participation strategies must provide opportunities for non-government actors to add to or influence the policy agenda through, for example, petitions or debate forums where issues of public concern not necessarily already on the mainstream political agenda can come to the fore.

• *Elections – promoting participation*

Given the low and falling election turnouts experienced in most countries at local and European elections, governments have a duty to be more involved in supporting the electoral process, at both an information and procedural level.

In general, governments are not involved in the dissemination of more than procedural information during election times - and for good reason. But now there is probably a need for rethinking how governments can support 'infomediaries' and what kind of role they should play in information provision during election times. It is likely that government agencies, and European institutions in particular, should be more active in the provision of election-related information which, while remaining non-partisan, should assist voters in evaluating their options. Whether directly providing voter-guide type information, or providing financial and information support to 'infomediaries' who will themselves offer this service, public authorities must be aware that information overload is a strong reason for voters not to engage in the process. Less controversially, governments can at least support or undertake 'Get out the vote' campaigns to raise awareness and voter registration.

• *Registration and voting*

E-voting is often mistaken for being the sum total of e-democracy. Governments can make voting easier and more convenient by offering a choice of voting channels from postal votes to in-person or online options. This may not raise voting turnout, but at least might reduce the practical barriers to not voting. By the same token, voter registration processes can be made more convenient through automating processes using new technologies, and allowing voter self-management of data options.

Representation Strategy

• *Modernising representation structures and processes*

Existing representation processes within parliament and government should be updated. This includes using new technologies to widen representation channels, using email, SMS and online interaction to connect citizens (or organised groups) with policy-makers and decision-makers. Parliamentarians can provide multi-channel opportunities for their voters to contact them and raise their concerns. (In non-constituency systems, elected representatives should be allocated 'constituencies' – which for example could be geographically organised, or grouped by policy areas.)

• *Encourage take-up of representation*

In order to stimulate public interest and involvement in political life, representation opportunities should be more widely promoted, particularly amongst traditionally under-represented groups. Governing authorities should build promotional campaigns, which could either be direct or via the relevant intermediary organisations or agencies that have most contact with these groups.

• *Active representation principles*

In addition to trying to encourage use of representation processes, a more active form of representation should be explored. This could take the form of information gathering (whether volunteered, solicited or researched) and needs assessments exercises for specific groups, with public posting of what their needs are assessed to be, and how these needs are met/intended to be met by policies. This kind of active demonstration of the representation process will not only improve the quality of policy and legislative developments but also encourage those who may have been misrepresented to speak out.

• *Quality control*

While many elected members believe that the electoral process provides sufficient quality control for their time in office, this is not enough. Citizens deserve to have a measure of how far their interests are being represented on different issues, and if not, why not. Parliamentarians should develop processes by which their voters can assess who is being represented by their decisions, and offer feedback in the form of satisfaction ratings.

Accountability

• *Clear attribution of responsibility*

The ability of citizens to hold their decision-makers to account for their actions is central to democratic governance. What often obscures this process is the lack of clarity or transparency in the division of responsibilities among parliamentarians, ministers or officials. This limits the ability of citizens (or more often, the media) to scrutinise their related actions. This problem is multiplied by multi-level governance and the complex distribution of responsibilities between European, national, regional and local authorities.

This strategy calls for more clarity of roles and responsibilities among governors (government and parliament included), which can come about, for example, through the innovative use of technology (e.g. in developing accountability-policy maps and searchable responsibility indexes).

• *Individual accountability practice guidelines*

While whole institutions or government department or agencies may be in the habit of producing annual reports for public scrutiny, individual elected members or ministerial level decision-makers are not always subject to sustained and equal scrutiny. Moreover, evaluating decisions and actions of different decision-makers over time or across regions (or countries) is difficult for citizens, because thus far, there is no standard accountability measure or process - either across governance levels or between countries. Basic guidelines on what is the appropriate information required for citizens to be able to hold their decision makers accountable, and how to do so, must be developed and adopted by elected and senior non-elected decision-makers at the European and national levels.

Evaluation

Continuous monitoring and evaluation will be essential for e-democracy activities to really have an impact, and thus evaluation must be a core component of this strategy.

• *Analysis of information*

At the outset, there should be a thorough evaluation of the various target audience groups and their needs, in order to develop citizen-focused information provision. As a corollary the effectiveness of subsequent information delivery must be measured. This includes an evaluation of how user-friendly the organisation, presentation and delivery of the information is, as well as the relevance and completeness of the information itself. The ultimate test will be an examination of levels of 'penetration' – that is, changing awareness and understanding of different issues or subjects, among the various audience groups, and an assessment of what the consequences of this are.

- *Evaluation of communications*

The take up and effectiveness of the various communications channels will also be evaluated, particularly with a view to examining depth and breadth of contributions in organised consultation exercises. This should also include an assessment of the quality of contributions and the overall outcomes of the debate, and the quality and levels of government response. At the same time, an evaluation of levels of integration of the various communications tools in the deployment across institutions and levels of government should also be undertaken.

- *Evaluation of active participation*

Evaluating the extent and outcomes of the various participation activities may be difficult – especially for those activities that are not government-assisted. However, an attempt should be made to measure the depth and breadth of participation, along with the accessibility of the various activities. At least the role of government or governing institutions can be assessed, both in promoting participation options and openness to citizens' initiatives. In terms of voting, turnout and choice of voting channel will be top-level indicators of success.

- *Evaluation of representation*

A straightforward means of evaluating the success of the representation strategy will be indicated by level and quality of take-up of the various representation channels. The outcomes of the active representation policy will be self-evident through the newly established quality control processes.

- *Evaluation of accountability*

While levels of accountability are difficult to assess, compliance with best practice guidelines will be at least a first step. The accountability of governing institutions and other democratic players should be assessed. An additional aspect will be the evaluation of the transparency levels of the different bodies, following on from the implementation of the transparency guidelines and processes incorporated in the information strategy.

Fig 2. Implementing the e-democracy strategy – examples of 'e' solutions

Information

- Online information, customisable for different audiences, with self-managed automatic email updates about issues of concern
- Self-service extranet for secondary information providers, and auto-publishing of content on external sites
- New editorial staff, and new online information to support e-consultations
- Online transparency index, detailing who is influencing decision-making and opportunities to participate
- Development of partnerships with online media providers and NGOs — bundling of related information from multiple authorities

Communication

- Online user satisfaction and feedback mechanisms, with auto-response procedures
- Online polling and opinion panels — for rapid and more deliberative feedback
- Online consultation toolbox, customisable for different audiences, accessible for local, national and European governing authorities
- Online hearings for parliamentary committees
- Consult an expert via email SMS for senior decision makers
- Online consultation register — with customised email updates
- Use of citizens and expert juries & panels

Participation

- Virtual commons — online community hall for public debate
- Targeted internet & email campaigns to promote activities in virtual commons, and associations
- Online hearings with MPs, ministers and officials on well supported public campaign issues
- E-petitions process for parliaments (& government policy departments)
- Technological infrastructure support to civil society — e.g. access to debate and consultation toolbox
- Online interactive voter guides and email motivational campaigns
- E-voting (via email, internet, SMS and iTV)

Representation

- Equip elected representatives to be more technologically capable
- Automatic processes to manage inbound email overload
- Integrated internet-email-telephone contact services
- Online and iTV surgeries
- Phone, email & SMS information campaigns to promote surgeries
- Providing online polls, debate forums, and consultation tools to enable more active representation
- Voter satisfaction surveys to monitor effectiveness of representation processes

Accountability

- Online responsibility index and search engine. For users to easily identify levels of government, departments and individuals responsible for specific policy areas or decisions.
- Elected and non-elected decision makers to publish online critical information in accordance with accountability guidelines

Implementation

Any strategy is only as good as its implementation. The strategy outlined here could in some ways be as much a conventional strategy for reinforcing and energising democracy, as an 'e' strategy. Indeed, if there were sufficient incentive and drive for governments to adopt democratic reform and modernisation, e-democracy would have become an add-on to an existing policy domain. Instead, the 'electronic' has become the driver for change in other areas, but nevertheless provides opportunities to do new things – creating new interactions and relationships. Fig. 2 above is an example of how this strategy may be implemented using the new technologies.

Conclusion

As we have seen, e-democracy is not the solution to the democratic deficit, but it can play an important role in addressing it. In developing this template for an e-democracy strategy, we have tried to be as comprehensive as possible, bearing in mind that the subject is still young and in formation. It is an ambitious project, entailing a thorough review of democratic institutions and processes. For the EU institutions, which are still young enough to have to prove themselves, this is an ideal challenge.

The Council, the media and the public at large
Norbert Schwaiger

Formally confidential - in practice open

From the beginning of the the European Communities in the 1950s the Council, invested by the Treaties as the main decision taker and legislator, has always been in practice a very open place for journalists who know their way around – in particular those based in Brussel. Notwithstanding the overall rule of confidentiality of its proceedings few arguments of any importance can remain hidden there for long. This has to do with the number of actors involved in Council activities: the Presidency, the fifteen Member States, the Commission and the Council Secretariat. All are possible sources of information.

There is – almost – always one or several of these actors who have a vested interest in explaining to the outside world what happened in the Council. But they do it in different ways, each according to their institutional position. For many years the distribution of roles among the actors was on the model of a classical intergovernmental conference.

Accordingly it was for the President of the Council to present to the media the formal decisions of the Council and the conclusions of its deliberations at regular press conferences during or at the end of Council sessions. The Council Secretariat – its press office – played a complementary role with the publication of press releases reflecting in as neutral and as objective a way as possible the outcome of Council proceedings.

In the execution of their tasks the Presidency and the Secretariat were confined, by virtu of the rule of confidentiality, to a rather formal role in the Council's information activities, leaving the more substantive information tasks to the Member States and to the Commission. The idea that the institution needed its own active information policy as well as institutional coherence and transparency developped only fairly recently and for a long time little was done to promote the corporate image of the institution as such or even to raise its outside visibility. There were almost no own publications presenting Council activities in an EU-wide context, or explaining the functioning and complexity of its proceedings. The annual activity reports were published only at the end of the year following the year to which they referred and were written in a largely sterile, bueaucratic language. TV coverage tended to show a national Minister attending and commenting on Council meetings rather than to portray the activities of the institution as such. At best TV stations might show short sequences of pictures of the building where the meetings take place and of the President currently chairing the Council.

Next there were the Member States who were generally very keen to explain to their own public opinion their positions taken in the Council proceedings and the results achieved, in particular as regards safeguarding national interests.

In this respect many national Ministers, who fly in to Brussels for Council meetings at best once a month for a maximum of one or two days after the bulk of the preparatory work has been done by their representatives on the spot, have hardly time to realise fully that they are part of an integrated legislative and political decision making body. They tend rather to apprehend EU policies and legislation decided by the Council as an integral part of their political realities at home and in terms of their own defence of national interests. This perception is underpinned by the fact that they are at the same time part of the decision-making process and also the main recipients of its results; in most cases their national administrations have to implement the legislation they have agreed in respect of their own population, generally in cooperation with or under supervision by the Commission. To most of them the Council – Brussels' – appears as a side-show of the national scene which remains their main theatre of operations. Logically there is a widespread tendency to claim positive' Council decisions for their country as a national and personnel success, while placing the blame for less favorable outcomes squarely on the shoulders of Brussels (i.e. the Union in general or more pointedly the Commission as the most – if not the only – visible EU actor there). With this trick Ministers can to some extent obscure in the eyes of their own public their responsability for participating in unpopular Council decisions.

There is also the Commission which participates in all Council sessions and its preparatory meetings at every level and which considers itself – in particular as far as EC matters are concerned, because of its right of initiative, its executive function, and its responsability as guardian of the treaties – entitled to contribute fully to information on Council activities.

The Commission has developped from the beginning a very active information policy, largely occupying the Brussels information market with frequent press conferences by Commissioners and daily briefings of its spokesman's group. It also uses very extensively information tools such as brochures, reports and periodical publications for both sectorial customers and the general public. In fact, its activities have been a major contributor to better public knowledge of EU policies, in particular for those directly interested in specific sectorial policies. On the institutional side it has fostered the impression in the public mind that the Commission *is* Brussels. Certainly it is the most visible of the European actors, with the consequence that Brussels is widely understood to be a synonym for the Commission. The reverse side of this medal, of course, is that Brussels stands for many as a place run by EU technocrats with no democratic legitimacy.

Each of these actors produces on its own initiative a substantial amount of information on almost all matters dealt with by the Council. Sometimes they find themselves in competition with each other or even taking antagonistic positions. By exploiting such situations it becomes very easy for investigative journalists to obtain complementary items of information from different sources adding up to the complete story on any possible subject. And the daily briefings by the Commission press service (formerly spokesman's group) at noon function as a rialto or stock exchange for journalists dealing in Community news from all institutions.

In addition there are a considerable number of news-letter publications which are most popular with Brussels insiders. They contribute as multipliers to spread information from different EU sources and thus allow journalists – as well as other interested people like lobbyists or diplomats – to be fully informed about Council activities without being obliged to shop around themselves for news.

How European information is distributed and perceived

The mass of information available – obtained either from open sources or from more discreet ones – is spread out across the world every day through a multitude of agency dispatches, articles and commentaries in the daily and periodical press, in general and specialised publications. Most of the radio and TV stations go on record also almost every day with information on European events in general and Council activities in particular.

Brussels has become – ahead of Washington, New York, London and Paris – the media location with the biggest concentration of international media, with more than 750 journalists accredited to the EU institutions.

There is however a big difference in the extent – and even more in quality – of coverage of Community affairs in the different media. This has substantial consequences for the level and accuracy of knowledge and understanding by different population groups in the Member States according to the media they receive.

Most of the important national newspapers and magazines offer wide-ranging and well documented information on EU affairs, putting their readers in a position to form themselves a reasoned opininon on Community events and policies. Those publications are most read by people with a certain level of education and with a general or sectoral interest in European politcal and economic developments.

At the other end of the spectrum, popular newspapers and those with narrow regional or local circulations have different objectives and normally reach a different kind of public. They mostly cover national or international news including Community affairs less exhaustively. The consequence is that their readers – i.e. the man in the street – is less well informed, and often in a less complete and balanced way, even though many of the decisions taken by the Council, now frequently together with the European Parliament , affect him directly in an increasing number of areas.

This gap can hardly be filled by TV and radio because they encounter serious problems in passing on to a wider public in accessible form substantial information on matters as complicated as European affairs. These media are good for short, breaking news items, highlighting in a few phrases or pictures the essentials of an event or a decision. But they are not usually good for in-depth, technical explanations. Not that they do not on occasion produce ambitious and well documented programmes, but these are mostly watched or listened to by the same type of viewers and listeners as read the more important and informative newspapers. The others find it easier to switch to more entertaining programmes.

An addidional handicap lies in the fact that most of the actors at EU level are hardly known outside their own country of origin and therefore are not suitable vectors for vulgarising EU information across borders. In each country there are relatively few public figures recognised as being a European' voice or face, and this limits the capacity of TV and radio to popularise complex stories from Brussels.

While the Council, despite its rule of confidentiality, was never a hermetically closed institution because of the number of sources available and the competition among them, the fact is that information about its proceedings, though widely available, often does not reach the man in the street, and when it does, it provokes frequently sceptical or even hostile reactions. This has to do rather with the spin given to the news by some of the sources it comes from, the way it is distributed, and the mind-set – often indifference or even hostility – with which it is received.

Frequently National media follow in their news coverage a similar scheme of presentation as certain Ministers. Starting from their perception of national interest and recording success or defeat in terms reported by the national Minister is often felt to be the best way to stimulate the interest of the reader, listener or viewer. Newsworthiness for EU events or decisions mainly depends on the significance of the subject for each national political scene and its public.

This way of presenting information on Council activities by certain sources and many of the media has certainly not helped to build a degree of allegiance or collective loyalty towards Community instituions, and towards the Council in particular, such as exists towards national and regional governments and parliaments. Rather it has contributed to maintain fences between different national public opinions, appealing to their different cultural, political and economic traditions and interests.

This presentation clearly did not match with repeated appeals by the Heads of State and Government in European Council declarations urging citizens to support their endeavours for the realisation of an ever closer union of the peoples of Europe'. And little was done to allow the citizens to apprehend behind the day-to-day business of selling Community affairs – largely determined by the national interest – the big design and the fondamental objectives of the European project.

This is all the more paradoxical as the EU's progressive geographical expansion from the original six to now fifteen and soon twenty-five Members States has been accompanied by a significant extension of its competences and responsabilities. In fact Member States, in order to respond better to the politcal and economic challenges of a rapidly globalizing world, have gone on to decide to pool their interests and policies well beyond the original areas – such as coal and steel, agriculture, foreign trade, nuclear research etc. – to include the completion of the internal market, with all that it implies and all that is connected to it, the creation of monetary union with the Euro as common currency, extensive cooperation in the field of justice and home affairs and the progressive shaping of a common foreign and security policy. Many of the common or coordinated policies developped over the years in these areas have confered rights and duties to the European citizens and have made a big impact on their lives. Such a development might have deserved greater efforts to make available comprehensive information and ensure that comprehensible explanation reach them in order to allow citizens to make their own politcal judgement on these affairs – not to force them to adhere to an ideal of European integration but at least to bring them to accept its necessity and, where possible, to support it.

Bringing the European Union closer to its Citizens: openness and transparency

The major turning point in the Council with respect to institutional transparency and the need to develop its own institutional information strategy came in the context of the Maastricht Treaty on European Union, and more specifically during the ratification process of this treaty. Indeed the danger of failure of ratification was looming in several Member States, and in the event some succeeded in passing the treaty through their Parliament or through a referendum only by a narrow margin. In Danmark it required a second consultation of the people after certain derogations had been re-arranged. Among the reasons identified by Heads of State and Government as responsible for this sitution was *inter alia* the lack of adequate information about the Maastricht treaty specifically and about European affairs in general.

This treaty itself in its article 1 enshrines the principle of openness whereby decisions are to be taken – in the EU – as openly as possible and as closely as possible to the citizen. Furthermore Declaration no. 17 annexed to its Final Act concerning the right for access to information states that transparency of the decision-making process would enhance the democratic caracter of the administration as well as the confidence of the public in Community institutions. It went on to ask the Commission to submit to the Council in the course of 1993 a report on measures aiming at better access for the public to information held by the institutions.

But it is with the conclusions of the European Councils of Birmingham (16 October 1992) and of Edinburgh (12 December 1992) on bringing the Community closer to its citizens and on transparency that a really new chapter in this domain was opened.

In the Birmingham declaration, the Heads of State and Government laid down four clear objectives:

- to demonstrate to our citizens the benefits of the Community and the Maastricht Treaty;

– to make the Community more open, to ensure a better informed public debate on its activities;

– to respect the history, culture and traditions of individual nations, with a clearer understanding of what Member States should do and what needs to be done by the Community;

– to make clear that citizenship of the Union brings our citizens additonal rights and protection without in any way taking the place of their national citizenship.

The Edinburgh conclusions identified a certain number of concrete measures for implementing the principle of openness:
- right of access to documents of all institutions,
- open sessions of the Council,
- better information in general on Council proceedings and results
- information in advance on forthcoming Council events by the Presidency and the Council Secretariat,
- better drafting and codification of Community legislation, and better coordination between EU institutions on these matters.

These conclusions aimed first of all at a psycho-political effect in the specific situation surrounding the difficultiues of ratification, showing that the highest political authority of the Communty, the European Council , was taking seriousely the concerns and fears of Member States' citizens. While the general objectives were formulated for all institutions, the concrete and practical measures focused clearly on the need to repair detected shortcomings in the openness of the Council as the main decision-taking body.

The new approach followed by the European Council clearly showed that, while in principle the rule of confidentiality was not called into question for core Council debates – necessary in particular for achieving compromises among Member States – this principle had been applied much too narrowly to date with respect to many aspects of Council proceedings , in particular to those relating to its legislative function.

This was particularly important at this moment as the treaty of Maastricht also innovated in the field of institutional power-sharing by introducing a legislative co-decision procedure which put the European Parliament for the first time on an equal footing with the Council with respect to law- making in the Community. At first glance, making the Council more transparent for EU citizens and introducing the legislative co-decision procedure between the Council and the European Parliament have nothing to do directly with each other, if it is not that both are the expression of the same will of the highest political authority of the Union to enhance the Council's democratic legitimacy. In practice, however, the two things are closely related, as legislative work by definition demands a high degree of openness in order to be understood – and hence accepted – by people affected by the decisions.

Therefore the new Council approach to transparency came just in time to help make the new co-decision procedure a success.

Transparency in practice

Implementing the objectives and measures formulated in the Birmingham and Edinburgh conclusions set in motion an ongoing process which has developped its own dynamism and tended to improve progressively the original provisions by learning from experience. The Council has been very active particularly with respect to the practical steps to enhance transparency for the benefit of the general public, through access to documents, opening up Council debates, improving the quality of drafting, simplifying and codifying Community legislation, etc. Its aim was to lay down the necessary procedural rules and conditions by the end of 1993 in order to be able to start applying these measures effectively from the bginning of 1994.

In June 1993 the Council began the process by adopting a resolution on the quality of the drafting of Community legislation.

In October 1993 the Council stated the steps it had already agreed on. In an inter-institutional declaration with the European Parliament and the Commission on democracy, transparency and subsidiarity it announced its intention

- to open some of its debates to the public,
- to publish common positions adopted under the co-operation and co-decision procedures along with the statement of reasons accompanying them,
- to publish records and explanations of its votes,
- to simplify and consolidate Community legislation in co-operation with the other institutions,
- to provide access to its archives,
- to improve its information to the media and the public on its current work and decisions as well as on its role and activities in general.

The other institutions stated equally the measures they had already taken or were in the process of taking.

In December 1993 the Council agreed on three further acts laying down the practical provisions for starting transparency measures from the beginning of 1994:
- a code of conduct with the Commission on common principles,
- an operational Council decision on access to documents,
- a decision containing revised rules of procedure of the Council which included provisions on public debates, making Council votes public, and a reference to the separate decision on access to documents.

On the basis of these acts and agreements the Council started to apply in practice the new transparency measures from the beginning of 1994. The start was rather slow and sometimes cumbersome, as on the one hand the public was not alerted in advance to the possibilities offered by the new facilities, and on the other hand those who had to apply these measures were on completely new ground and had to learn by doing it.

A positive element in this context was that the launching of the transparency measures coincided with rapid developments in information technology. The extensive use of new technology eased considerably the search for appropriate solutions at least for some of the more technical communications problems encountered. The installation and interconnection of numerous web-sites and data-bases throughout the Community institutions, including the Council and successive Presidencies, was very helpful in this respect.

a. Access to documents

Public access to Council documents proved from the beginning to be the most promising in terms of transparency gains for the public but also the measure which needed the greatest attention and care for its implementation.

The code of conduct and the Council decision re-stated the principle that the public should have the widest possible access to documents (defined as any written text whatever its medium which contains existing data). Both acts, however, contain a list of exceptions concerning:
- the protection of the public interest (public security, international relations, monetary stability, court proceedings, inspections and investigations);

- the protection of the individual and of privacy;
- the protection of commercial and industrial secrecy;
- the protection of the Community's financial interests;
- the protection of confidential documents supplied by third persons or Member States.

Access may also be refused in order to protect Council's interest in the confidentiality of its proceedings.

The procedure starts with a written application to the Council Secretariat with sufficiently precise information to allow the document(s) to be identified. The answer was to be given originally within one month by the Secretariat. Since 30 May 2001 this period has been reduced to fifteen working days. If the answer is positive the applicant can either consult the document on the spot or have a copy sent – in principle – at his own cost. If the answer of the Secretariat is negative the applicant had equally one month originally – since 30 May 2001 fifteen working days – to make a confirmatory application to the Council as such to ask for the negative position to be reconsidered. The Council decision on that must be taken – since 30 May 2001 – within a further fifteen working days (originally one month), and if it remains negative the grounds must be given and the decision must indicate the means of redress that are available, i.e. complaints to the EU Ombudsman and judicial proceedings.

One of the basic problems encountered at the very beginning was the identification of the documents requested; all too often the Council was confronted here with very vague or general descriptions demanding considerable research to clarify the request. But this difficulty contributed to give birth to another new transparency instrument which has already proved to be very useful for a great number of people in and outside the institutions, viz. the creation – by Council decision of March 1998 – of a public register, accessible by electronic means, for all Council documents (titles, dates and reference numbers), with only a few exceptions regarding highly classified documents.

This register has been developed also as the key site for publication of Council documents which are free for direct release (such as agendas for Council meetings and most of its preparatory bodies) as well as for texts which are for publication anyway or for which publication has been authorised either on a single request or by a generally applicable decision. The steady increase of documents which enter in the category for automatic release has reduced considerably the scope of application for the special access procedure to Council documents

By the end of December 2002, the register referred to 375, 154 documents, across all official languages; the content of 168, 647 of these documents could be accessed directly. In 2002, approximately 900, 000 persons logged on to the internet site of the register and consulted in all 4,600,000 pages.

With regard to the access procedure in general, some difficulties encountered stemmed from the fact that a limited number of people - including some journalists – tested the limits of the new system both quantitatively and qualitatively. At times they made applications causing excessive or disproportionate costs by the number of documents requested or they unduly repeated requests which had been refused. In some cases they asked for documents which fell under the stated exceptions concerning the protection of the public interest (public security, court proceedings etc.) or of the protection of Council proceedings for reasons of safeguarding in particular the confidentiality of Member States' negotiating positions.

Some of these cases came to the EU Court of Justice, respectively to the Court of First Instance, where the Council did not always emerge as the winner. But the judgements of the Court have offered valuable clarifications on how to arrive at a better weighting of interests between the applicants and the Council, between improved access and protecting the confidentiality of Council proceedings or the public interest. And following disputes with applicants which went to the Court or the Ombudsman, another instrument which has allowed greater openness in the release of documents has been developed, namely the partial release of documents, distinguishing between sensitive and non-sensitive parts.

Overall the scheme works well; the number of applications has steadily increased and a certain degree of standardisation in the Council's management makes it possible to cope with the increasing number without too many difficulties. All those involved in the running of the scheme confirm its practical usefulness and an increased awareness that greater transparency was necessary. The number of applications in fact jumped from 70 in 1994 to 2,491in 2002.

The 70 applications in the first year covered 443 documents, of which only 378 fell under the scope of the scheme. Of these 222 received a favourable reply i.e. 58,7 per cent; of these, 185 directly by the Council Secretariat and 37 decided by the Council in response to 16 confirmatory applications.

The 2,491 requests in 2002 (effective reference period 3. 12. 2001 to 31. 12. 2002) covered 10,330 documents of which 9,114 were supplied directly by the Council Secretariat (8,017 released in full and 1,097 in part); a further 89 were released by the Council in response to 44 confirmatory applications. The number of documents refused was 1,127. That gives an overall document access rate of 77 per cent counting only the documents released in full and 89,1 per cent when adding documents partially released.

It is interesting to explore where the applications come from. In 2002 students and researchers came top for initial requests (23,5 per cent), followed by the commercial and industrial sector (14,5 per cent), pressure groups (13 per cent) and lawyers (10,5 per cent), while 22 per cent remained unidentified. For confirmatory applications students and researchers were top again (31,8 per cent); second come journalists (18,2 per cent), a sector which for initial requests represented only 2 per cent, indicating perhaps that they were looking for more sensitive material.

As for the geographical spread of initial requests, Belgium – seat of most of the EU Institutions – was first (27,5 per cent) followed by Germany (13 per cent) and the United Kingdom (9,5 per cent), while the UK came easily top for confirmatory applications (40,9 per cent).

Finally the frequency of sectors requested showed Justice and Home Affairs top (24,5 per cent), then Internal Market (14,5 per cent), Economic and Monetary Affairs (10,5 per cent), External Relations and CFSP (8,5 per cent) and finally Environment (8 per cent).

On 30 May 2002 the European Parliament and the Council adopted a new regulation regarding public access to documents of the two institutions and the Commission under the legislative co-decision procedure. The new regulation does not alter substantially the basic elements of the original Council regulation as described above, but it brings a number of practical adaptations based on experience of the previous regulation.

The new regulation has in particular shortened the time scale for the whole scheme. The time limit for initial replies by the Institutions to requests for documents, for the introduction of confirmatory applications by citizens and for the answers to those requests are all reduced now from one month to fifteen working days. There is a possibility of an extension, however, for a further fifteen days when an Institution encounters difficulties in producing its reply within the first fifteen days (e.g. a great number of documents or long and complicated documents requested).

The new rules also integrate a number of elements developed under the previous regulation, such as the public register of documents for all three institutions, including the possibility for using it to make certain documents directly accessible or for indicating where the document is located. It redefines also more precisely the exceptions justifying refusal of access, generally in a more balanced and therefore more user-friendly way. It introduces special rules for classified documents for both their entry in the register and for their accessibility. It introduces a distinction between legislative and other documents and charges the Council Secretariat to make legislative documents directly accessible as widely and as early as possible unless one of the specific exceptions explicitly applies. Finally the new regulation establishes an inter-institutional committee to examine best practice, address possible conflicts and discuss future developments on public access to documents.

b. Open debates

With regard to open Council sessions, the rules of procedure of the Council mentioned above provided for regular open policy debates in the General Affairs Council and the ECOFIN Council on the six-monthly work programmes of the Presidencies and, if appropriate, on the Commission's annual work programme. In addition it was left up to the Council to decide unanimously on a case by case basis to open up for the public debates on important issues affecting the interest of the Union or on important new legislative proposals . The formula

'Open Council Sessions' is to be understood as re-transmission by audio-visual means, namely into a (press-)room inside the Council building and via TV networks, in practice most often the Commission facility Europe by Satellite which can then be picked up as required by other TV broadcasters.

In the beginning, open debates enjoyed a curiosity value with TV stations. Several tested full time transmissions lasting up to two hours in their pre-noon programmes, but they became rapidly disillusioned about the attractiveness of prepared interventions read out by Ministers which, in addition in their translation by interpreters, lost all spontaneity. Journalists found debates on the six-months Presidency and annual Commission work programmes sufficiently interesting to attend in numbers of around 150 to 200 as they could expect a real debate on work priorities and on possible results for the months or year ahead. But as far as topical debates were concerned, apart from a limited number of specialists, the majority of the press found them rather dull, because stage managed and rarely on hot subjects.

For the occasional TV transmissions there are no programme ratings available but viewer numbers must be very limited in general terms, even if interested segments of the public watching specific political channels may be reached.

Bringing the public at large into the Council was a somewhat slower operation. The new possibility for the public to attend Council meetings was not made known at all outside the EU institution by media reports. Only after some publicity specifically directed to universities and through the Council web-site did some individuals and a few groups start to attend. Their number has increased very slowly.

Despite the relative lack of popular interest – attendance at these topical debates rarely reached 100 persons – successive Presidencies have regularly presented their programme for open debate in the Council, generally six topics in different specific policy areas in addition to the two general debates on the working programmes.

Following the conclusions of the Seville European Council in June 2002, the focus of the scheme has been changed towards making Council deliberations on legislative matters decided by co-decision the centrepiece. For that, at the beginning of its term, each Presidency, after consulting the Commission, submits a list of the most important legislative proposals ahead to the Council for approval. The presentation by the Commission of these proposals and the ensuing debate are made open to the public. In addition, the vote on legislative acts is also open to the public as well as the final deliberations leading to that vote and the accompanying explanations by Ministers of their positions. The results of the votes are indicated by visual means (electronic board). But, while the intention may be good, the practicalities leave much to be desired as far as broadcasters are concerned. The Council finds it very difficult to indicate even approximately when the votes may take place, and well nigh impossible to hold Ministers to any time – however approximate – that has been announced.

Furthermore, the new Seville provisions have replaced the two six-monthly debates on the Presidencies' work programmes by one debate on the Council's annual operational programme and – if appropriate – on the Commission's work programme. At least one further public debate on important new legislative proposals is to be held and others can be added by the Council deciding by qualified majority.

The new scheme is still in the testing phase, but there are already doubts whether it will prove much more attractive to the public than the original one. But the message is clearly that openness should focus in particular on the legislative work of the Council.

c. Record of votes and connected measures

According to the Council's rules of procedure, votes in Council shall be made public when the Council is acting as legislator. Similarly, votes are to be made public when the Council in the context of its legislative co-operation with the European Parliament adopts a common position in the co-decision or co-operation procedure, or when the vote takes place in the Conciliation Committee. In other cases the Council may decide to publish the votes at the request of one of its members. In cases concerning the Common Foreign and Security Policy or Justice and Home Affairs, however, this decision must be taken unanimously. The publication appears in the press release of the session in which the vote was taken.

This scheme has been extended progressively to include explanations of votes by Ministers and statements written into the minutes of the Council – when it acts as legislator – made by the Council, the Commission or Member States. This allows for them to be made public in order to make the voting process and the final stage of Council proceedings leading to the adoption of a legal act as transparent as possible. The fact that such explanations or statements have been made is recorded in the press release of the Council Secretariat and made available by electronic means. The treaty of Amsterdam has confirmed the whole instrument in its article 207.

d. Quality of drafting Community legislation

The June 1993 Council Resolution on this subject, already mentioned above, laid down a set of guidelines as criteria against which Community texts should be checked as they are drafted: i.e. use of clear, simple, concise and unambigious wording; avoiding unneccessary abreviations, Community jargon and excessively long phrases, imprecise references or too many cross references to other texts; inconsistency between provisions of the same text and with other existing texts, as well as a number of methodical and formal provisions.

This resolution, while it is not legally binding, prepared the ground for the adoption in December 1999 of an Inter-institutional Agreement (which is equally not legally binding) between the European Parliament, the Council and the Commission. This established in greater detail, on the basis of the same principles, common guidelines for the internal use of each of the three institutions. The Agreement is addressed to all those in the institutions who are involved in the drafting of legislative acts, in order to make those acts transparent and readily understandable by the general public and by economic operators. These qualities are also a prerequisite for the proper implementation and uniform application of Community legislation in member States. Respecting the guidelines is intended to contribute to greater legal certainty, a principle that the European Court of Justice considers a crucial aspect of the legal order of the Community.

e. Improving general information for the media and the public

With regard to improving information on current Council activities and its role in general, successive Presidencies have stepped up their information activities both in their national capital and in Brussels by increasing the number of staff affected to this task and by installing special web-sites for Presidency/Council information. These sites are linked to the web-site of the Council Secretariat. Increasing importance has been taken over recent years in the CFSP area by the 'Presidency Statements on behalf of the EU' which are agreed by all partners in the CFSP network and which represent the official position of the EU on international events and situations. They serve at the same time also to inform through the media domestic and international public opinion. These statements are published simultaneously in Brussels and in the Presidency's capital. A special role is also played by the Secretary General/High Representative for CFSP in the formulation and day-to-day running of this policy which he and his spokesperson assume also by regularly informing the press about his activities.

Successive Presidencies also give regular pre-Council briefings for the Brussels press corps to explain the issues on Council agendas as well as possible/expected outcomes. The Council Secretariat Press Office assists the Presidency in these briefings and produces for the same occasion background notes with detailed information on the state of play of the different topics on the agenda. The Press Service has also been encouraged to continue its efforts to put as much substantive information as possible in the press releases which it produces after Council sessions and other Council events (such as Association and Co-operation Councils and other meetings with third country representatives, etc.).

In addition, inside the Council Secretariat a new Information Policy, Transparency and Public Relations Service has been set up which handles the management of the Access to documents scheme as well as the public register for Council documents and the information pages of the web-site of the Council Secretariat. In this it works together with the Press Office. It also answers a large number of information requests, most of which come in by e-mail and which are answered in the same way. This service is also responsible for the edition of useful Council texts and explanatory brochures, such as the collection 'Basic texts on transparency concerning the activities of the Council' and a 'Guide to information in the Council' and many more.

As for the readiness of Member States to contribute to information on Council activities as a matter of common interest, most have responded positively to the repeated appeals over the last ten years by the European Council and the General Affairs Council to take up this collective responsibility. Several have given a new stimulus and to some extent a re-orientation to their own information policies. This positive tendency is sustained by numerous obligations and opportunities to work together on specific transparency instruments, such as access to documents, where Member States decide in the Council – after preparation by the working group for information and the Committee of Permanent Representatives – on the confirmative applications for documents. Similarly they prepare decisions about open debates and the topics to be covered. Ministers also have the experience of performing in these debates, as do senior civil servants in seminars for the exchange of ideas and experience for better co-operation between the different EU and national information services. They also attend co-ordination meetings between those responsible for information in the EU institutions and national administrations to discuss concrete actions such as media campaigns or common publications on EU matters. This co-operation gets increasing attention in particular in the run-up to the European elections in 2004.

The centrifugal and traditional forces in the Council information practice, as described above, have not simply disappeared overnight. Indeed, the underlying causes which gave rise to them have not either. But they are now increasingly being counterbalanced by a sense of joint responsibility and action taken by all actors – national and European – for more institutional openness and transparency.

Final remarks

It is still too early to assess whether the efforts to increase openness and transparency in the Council as an institution have made a positive impact on public opinion in the different Member States. For this the turnout of voters in the upcoming elections for the European Parliament in 2004 will present a suitable test, showing whether the disappointing 1999 results in voter participation can possibly be improved.

In any case the policy of openness and transparency in the Council should be developed further as the measures already implemented have proved their usefulness for all those who have a general or sectoral interest and need to follow Council activities, be it for political or economic reasons. These people no longer need to depend on more or less fortuitous channels for getting large parts of the information they need. They now have a right to know which documents exist, to apply for access to those documents, to learn the results of votes and read or hear voting explanations in the Council.

The European Union has reached a point where the level of transfers of competencies from the Member States to the European institutions affect almost all areas of the lives of European citizens. To confer on this legislative process the necessary democratic legitimacy to ensure acceptance by European citizens, these same citizens need as large as possible a right of access to information on how they are governed, how the institutions use their competencies in the common interest. The Heads of State and Government realised that this was needed in the light of the difficulties surrounding the ratification of the Maastricht Treaty. They have shown since then their determination to make openness and transparency of the Union one of their major objectives, and they have built on that concept step by step with concrete measures. This process has developed its own intrinsic dynamism which has contributed to the development of a more general spirit and climate of openness affecting all areas of information and communication in the Council. That has spread more widely across EU institutions and among the Member States.

In the Treaty of Maastricht they followed the same road of extending democratic legitimacy of the Union's activities in the legislative field by giving to the European Parliament – finally – the competence of co-decision with the Council. The road has been long to reach this result – as it was for that of the openness and transparency process – from the rather decorative and consultative role which the original treaties had reserved to the 'Parliamentary Assembly' composed then of delegated Members of national Parliaments. However, many Member States had seen from the beginning the potential of this Parliamentary Assembly as one of the democratic anchors of the whole integration process. They did not miss the opportunity to develop it, slowly but steadily following the increase of substantive competencies and responsibilities of the EU and to some extent in parallel to the extension of its geographical scope .

The road towards legislative co-decision led through the attribution of substantive (even if limited) co-decision powers on the Community budget (1970 and 1975), direct elections by universal suffrage (1979), and the introduction by the Single European Act of the co-operation procedure and assent procedure (1987), the first for some legislative matters and the second for the ratification of accession and association treaties.

Then with the Maastricht treaty the European Parliament's role took on a new quality as the co-decision procedure put it for the first time in the legislative process on an equal footing with the Council. This procedure now applies – since the Treaties of Amsterdam and Nice – to most of the areas where the Union enjoys legislative powers. After a certain running-in period it is now working smoothly and has led to a new type of relationship between the two institutions, characterised by a spirit of dialogue – also involving the Commission – in all phases of the procedure. A sense of shared responsibility has developed favouring the search for compromise throughout the whole procedure, particularly in the final stage, when the Conciliation Committee is called to meet if there has been no agreement at an earlier stage.

The development of this positive climate surrounding the running of the co-decision procedure has been favoured by the parallel move in which the Council was engaged with respect to transparency and openness. This focused on the legislative domain in general and the co-decision procedure in particular, and transparency and openness instruments such as the public register and the right of access to Council documents, publishing votes and voting explanations on common positions in the co-decision procedure and in the Conciliation Committee assisted this process. The development of a culture of openness on legislative matters within the Council towards the public, such as existed already in the Parliament, was a further element contributing to a sense of equality between both institutions in the context of this procedure.

The search for greater openness of the EU, and in particular for enhanced democratic legitimacy in its legislative action, was also a determining factor when the European Council meeting in Laeken in Belgium in December 2001 decided to convene the European Convention on the future of Europe. It asked the Convention to draw up proposals on three subjects:
- how to bring citizens closer to the European design and European Institutions;

- how to organise poilitics and the European political area in an enlarged Union;
- how to develop the Union into a stabilising factor and a model in the new world order.

The Convention presented to the European Council in Thessaloniki in June 2003 a Draft Treaty establishing a Constitution for Europe. This document contained proposals which respond to all the questions put to the Convention in the Laeken Declaration. In the chapter concerning the democratic life of the Union, which deals with the principles of democratic equality and representative democracy, it contains a set of basic rules concerning transparency in the proceedings of the Union Institutions and develops further the principle of participatory democracy.

In order to promote good governance and ensure the participation of civil society, it restates the principle that the Union Institutions, bodies and agencies shall conduct their work as openly as possible. The Council of Ministers, like the European Parliament, shall meet in public when examining and adopting legislative proposals. Any citizen of the Union and any natural or legal person established in a Member State shall have a right of access to documents of the Union Institutions, bodies and agencies. Details are to be laid down both in a 'European law' and in the rules of procedure of each entity.

With respect to participatory democracy the Convention proposes that the Union Institutions shall

- by appropriate means give citizens and representative associations the opportunity to make known and publicly exchange their views on all areas of Union action;
- maintain an open, transparent and regular dialogue with representative associations and civil society.

The Commission for its part shall carry out broad consultations with parties concerned in order to ensure that the Union's actions are coherent and transparent. A completely new instrument provides that 'no less than one million citizens coming from a significant number of Member States may invite the Commission to submit any appropriate proposal on matters where citizens consider that a legal act is required for the purpose of implementing this Constitution'. Specific procedures and conditions required for such a citizens' initiative shall be determined by a 'European law'.

If the Intergovernmental Conference meeting from late 2003 endorses these constitutional provisions, and when, after ratification by all Member States, they enter into force, the Union will finally have at its disposal all the tools necessary to make the building of Europe – which started largely as an enterprise of governments and diplomats – into a proper matter of its citizens.

EbS: the Commission's flagship
Anthony O'Donnell

Europe by Satellite – EbS – is a TV news agency, a service providing EU-related TV pictures to media professionals since 1995. Run by the European Commission, its coverage extends to every institutional player in the European integration process.

Free of charge, it has become a vital one-stop shop for broadcasters wanting to cover the multi-faceted, ever-changing European Union. With the calendar of EU events becoming ever more full, EbS's online services have also become valuable to journalists of the written press who are finding it harder and harder to cover events often in different cities at the same time. By the same token, it has become an indispensible tool for the army of EU camp followers – politicians, academics, lawyers and lobbyists – who like to be as informed as possible – and as quickly as possible – about new developments.

The year of the new service's birth was marked by the emergence of several factors which were to prove significant in the launch of the EbS project. Opinion polls – following the previous year's record low turn-out for the European Parliamentary elections – persistently told a tale of public ignorance of, and indifference to, the European project, while the recent enlargement of the Union to include Finland, Austria and Sweden merely increased the task of harassed information officers and spokesmen. And if all that was not enough, the charismatic and controversial Jacques Delors had gone and taken his unfailing newsworthiness with him.

The Commission had to face up both to a new life style and a growing information deficit. But communications tools that had shown great potential for a decade or so were breaking through to new levels of sophistication and speed.

Early in 1995 the Commission was busy discharging one of Delors' last commitments –that of organising for the first (and so far only) time a G7 meeting that looked at the challenges of the fast-expanding information society. The accompanying exhibition's demonstrations of the potential of the Web, cybernetics, robotics and of then new concepts like teleworking and telemedicine – in short, the awesome possibilities and global reach of the new information technology – inspired many of those who saw them. A number of EU officials were among those confirmed in their intention to ensure that their institutions reacted promptly to take the new developments on board both practically and politically.

The mission to explain European integration was no less urgent than ever, and now these new media offered promising methods of delivering facts and pictures both more quickly and more directly. To begin a satellite TV service which was soon to be backed up by the globally accessible Web was, in fact, quite a modest step in response to some of the marvels on view in Brussels in the February of 1995.

At the same time a significant shift in the style of coverage of the EU was happening, in line with change in the nature of the European media itself. There was less emphasis on the erudite article in the broadsheet newspapers, and more electronic journalism. 24-hour-a-day satellite-driven rolling news had arrived .

The obvious advantage was a fast and plentiful supply of video images, but among the disadvantages came a marked reduction in the time available to commentators for analytic reflection on new developments, and also a limit on the possibilities for following-up and expanding the story. Editors and executives meanwhile were faced with lower budgets but also audiences who had acquired a greater appetite for pictures of what was going on. These factors created a climate receptive to the service offered by EbS.

The debate about Europe was no longer confined to initiated experts – the EU's profile had grown to an extent that ensured that

EU affairs became a significant part of the general news agenda, read and watched by the general public as well as the Euro cognoscenti. This wider audience preferred the broadcast media. The Union's own polling service – Eurobarometer – consistently confirmed it.

And the press corps meeting everyday in the EC HQ in Brussels was growing bigger – equalling the numbers of journalists covering the White House and Capitol Hill in Washington. Representing as they did – and do – a whole range of media with differing agendas, this big press corps is less homogeneous than their US colleagues. Some are technical rather than political, specialising in environmental or agricultural subjects or concentrating on enlargement or competition matters. Covering the big picture in a comprehensive kind of way – so that there iss something for everybody – was done by a few specialist agencies, working in Brussels and through the written word. But few covered the European project on its own terms, let alone on television, and a theory grew that a pan-European outlook could provide an objective and comprehensive TV coverage which would make a new and vigorous contribution to the editorial mix.

Early Initiatives

One early pioneering concept was that of *Epitel* (or European Public Information by TV) which was floated in†1990. Backed by several European-based non-governmental organisations, it aimed to emulate the specialist Washington cable channel C-Span that covers political events in and around Congress, but it could not be progressed at the time – despite support from the European Parliament – because of technical and bureaucratic difficulties.

The first pan-European broadcaster to make a real impact on the screen was *EuroNews*. The channel was born in 1993, partly from the European Broadcasting Union's recognition of the need to reflect the increasing scale of EU integration, partly in admiring imitation of CNN, whose impressive worldwide coverage of the first Gulf War provoked much thought among European broadcasters. It began operations near Lyon with a small but dedicated team that mainly recycled the pictures of other newsrooms. Public broadcast budgets were under pressure and *Euronews'* capacity to commission its own coverage was slow to develop. But the existence of EbS would soon prove to be be a major help to *Euronews'* coverage of the EU scene.

EbS was not an overnight creation. The history of TV in the European institutions is long, even if the profile or importance accorded it down the years has not always been as high as hindsight shows it should have been. The written press, particularly in its broadsheet form, was for many years the preoccupation of EC information officers. Lengthy articles and specialist correspondents lent themselves more readily to the complex affairs of European integration than picture-based three minute items in the TV news bulletins.

But from the very beginning of the EU project's long march there was at least a determination that the key moments in the process should be recorded on film and stored for future generations. So the principal mission of the fledgling audiovisual department of the Commission was to capture significant moments on celluloid, or acquire existing footage from other sources to make good any gap in the historical record. But the schedule was seldom full in the early years. For instance, during one week in 1979 an award of an honorary degree from a Belgian university to the then Commission President Jenkins was the only event on the filming schedule.

But the nature of both the EU institutions and of television stations began to change. As the former grew more important and the latter more competitive and more numerous, the audio-visual department of the Commission found itself providing pictures on a much more regular basis to the electronic media, a media which, by now converted to video rather than film-based pictures, was becoming much speedier, more flexible and much more electronic.

During the seventies,there was a growing trend towards the use of news exchanges, a sort of bring-and-buy sale for news pictures. Public service TV companies, who had already linked up their resources through the Geneva-based European Broadcasting Union, led the trend through the Eurovision News Exchange.

By 1980, after the first direct elections, the European Parliament decided to establish its own dedicated audiovisual unit in recognition of the prime popular importance of the broadcast media, and the difficulty of attracting its attention when based in three separate locations in Brussels, Luxembourg and Strasbourg. By the end of the decade this unit had tripled the broadcast coverage given to the EU's only directly-elected body and not only guaranteed gavel-to-gavel coverage of the EP's plenary session to the regular or casual broadcaster, but also coverage of some of the meetings of the key specialist committees. As with the pictures offered from much earlier in the EU's development by the Commission, there was no charge to the news programme concerned, and the journalist reporting the event could choose precisely what material he or she wanted to use or to ignore. The great disincentive, however, remained the costs of broadcast-quality links between Strasbourg and the home TV station when the report was completed, because for that the broadcaster did have to pay.

Brussels, the Capitals and the Regions

The general trend indicated a growing interest in EU picture material, linked, for the idealistic observer, with the growing profile and powers of the European institutions, but for the cynic, to a long term decline in production budgets. In truth, both played their part in growing TV coverage, together with the move by TV news itself to the centre stage of journalism in Europe. By the end of the Eighties, the case for a correspondent in Brussels was unanswerable for most of the major media players with budget enough to set up an office. There just always seemed to be a story.

But the mere existence of the biggest press corps in the world on the doorstep of the Institutions did not solve every problem faced by EU information officers of Brussels.

For one thing, the deliberations of Brussels in one form or another were beginning to influence the work of journalists based throughout the European Union, and there was only so much they could learn during the occasional facilities trip to the Belgian capital. Political, agricultural, environmental, technical or even media specialists, more and more they needed regular updating on how the latest decisions of the EU affected their special subjects.

Mirroring the political interest in subsidiarity was an increasing emphasis on Europe's regions and their distinct identities, and a growth in local and regional broadcasters. The reliability of TV pictures broadcast by satellite had by then become dependable enough, not just for the domestic viewer but also for the widespread distribution of pictures good enough for re-broadcast, giving Commission broadcast managers the option of complementing – if not entirely replacing –

the onerous and expensive system of making broadcast quality tapes of pictures and then distributing them physically. A competitive market had also emerged of satellite service providers who could offer a viable transponder to take and provide a signal.

Increasing Institutional Transparency

Inside the institutions, an increasing accent on transparency was also providing more and more public events that could provide live TV proceedings.

The European Parliament, whose plenary had by1995 been televised for twelve years without incident, save one at the outset when a British Conservative MEP who was chairing the session ordered the TV lights to be cut because they were disturbing proceedings, was the prime example. But the European Council meeting in Edinburgh at the end of 1992 also wrote a general commitment to increased transparency into its conclusions, even promising open sessions of the Council of Ministers' meetings in Brussels.

The Commission, meanwhile, had been offering integral video recordings of its press conferences, with due respect to 'off-the-record' passages, since the end of 1991. At that stage is was forced to move to the Breydel building when its Berlaymont HQ was obliged to close because of the health risk posed by the excessive quantities of asbestos it contained.

By then all the elements were in place for a 'one-stop-shop' providing live TV coverage and access to extensive library video. A discussion paper preceding the EbS launch described the new venture as an'delivery system and a dedicated European Union news agency'. Its founding managers saw 'three important principles behind the foundation of the channel: the creation of one unique source for all live pictures from the EU, a means of distributing news pictures and archive footage appropriate to the agenda of events, and a permanent tool for broadcasting important live EU events.'

The sole issue remaining to be resolved was technical; whether the transponder for the service was to be rented on a twenty- four hour a day basis – and this proved to be the option offering best value for money. That discussion paper also suggested a further use for the satellite as a vehicle for interactive press conferences – linking Brussels and any point within the EbS footprint to enable key players to talk news, policy and process directly with any group of journalists or other interested players. Full broadcast quality pictures are provided, enabling clips to be edited for TV news bulletins subsequently.

The Current Situation

Now, in 2003, eight years after its debut broadcast, EbS offers transmissions that are available round-the-clock, on Internet, live and, during the week following the broadcast, as video on demand. Its sixteen audio channels enable coverage of multi-lingual live events, or the distribution of radio programmes, by satellite or by the Internet. One development with significant implications for news editors hard up both for facilities and resources is the recent availability of short broadcast quality video through the Internet as an alternative picture source to satellite reception.

The introduction of EbS picture streaming onto the Europa internet site (www.europa.eu.int/comm/ebs) have given users a bigger picture that is better synchronised with an improved sound quality. It comes with a choice of twelve audio channels, and site hits indicate that 92 per cent of users follow events in the language of their choice, while the rest stay with the original sound. 72 per cent of visitors to the site live in the European Union, 10 per cent from the future member states and 18 per cent from the rest of the world. The number of hits received from outside the EU tripled during the first six months of 2003. From among the future member states Poland, Hungary, Lithuania and the Czech Republic were the most prominent, while 20 per cent of recorded hits came from the United States of America.

Regular users of the satellite service include big pan-european stations such as *CNBC* and *EuroNews*, whose live EU events coverage is a retransmission of EbS. They include, too, regional TV stations throughout Europe and beyond, prohibited from covering events with their own staff by the cost of maintaining a camera crew in Brussels or in Strasbourg. Its pictures are also a major source for the big international TV agencies such as *Reuters* or *APTV*, and for the specialised TV channels like the parliamentary channel *Phoenix* in Germany or a minority broadcaster like Sweden's *Open channel*. And it has moved beyond Europe – offering hour-long summaries of its weekly broadcasts which are aimed at users in America, in Asia, in

Africa, Australia and Latin America.

In the first half of the current year, two major milestones in the history of the EU were broadcast in large measure by EbS. First, came the end of negotiations for the enlargement of the European Union with the ten new member states from Central and Eastern Europe and the Baltics. Then, at the end of the work of the constitutional convention led by Valéry Giscard d'Estaing came the handing-over of the draft project to Heads of State and Government in Thessalonika, followed by the beginning of the Inter-Governmental Conference in Rome in October 2004. EbS followed all these proceedings closely.

EbS also provided intensive coverage of major European Councils,including the meeting of EU leaders on the Iraq crisis – as well as the EU-Russia summit and other major international gatherings like the recent G8 in Evian.

Monitoring Results

How then to evaluate the impact of so singular a venture as Europe-by-Satellite? Monitoring comprehensively a service with so large a potential outreach is clearly an expensive proposition in times of budgetary constraint for the European institutions. But

The most recent available study was carried out in March 2003 at the time of the Brussels European Council – a Council which took place on the day war was declared in Iraq, an event which substantially altered the summit's agenda. The evaluation concentrated only on EbS use at that time in Denmark, Spain and France and attempted to identify the presence of pictures provided through EbS, and the lenght of time on air.

Fourteen channels were followed, eight of them public service broadcasters. The number of news items screened totalled 153, and 116 featured pictures broadcast from the summit by EbS – roughly 75 per cent. In terms of length used, those pictures made up nearly 50 per cent of the average item. A small and partial test of usage certainly – just a few of the stations who habitually use EbS pictures were tested at a time of unusually concentrated interest in EU affairs – but it suggests that those users monitored at that time were not only frequently, but also intensively reliant on the EbS source. The monitoring report said

'It is possible to put forward the hypothesis that certain channels ... would have completely abstained from broadcasting pictures of the summit if EbS did not exist.'

Current figures show that, in terms of total hours broadcast, a third deal with the European Parliament, a third is concerned with the Commission, and a fifth covers Council business – a proportion that has remained relatively constant over the past few years. 15 per cent of hours broadcast during 2003 dealt with the proceedings of the Convention drafting the new Constitution. The rest of EbS air time is regularly given over to coverage of significant judgements from the Court of Justice, press conferences from the European Central Bank, or excerpts from plenary sessions of the Committee of the Regions.

The programming is set on a weekly basis and planned at a meeting with representatives of the contributing institutions present. The schedule is then posted on the Internet for the benefit of users. Transmissions of live events are determined by their timing, while the news exchange material comes at fixed times each day: at 08h.00, 11h.30, 14H.30, 17h.30 and at 19h.00 with special contributions added when necessary. Video stockshots are broadcast just before or just after the news transmissions. Interactive briefings are scheduled between 09h.00 and 11h.00, or between 13h.00 and 16h.00.

EbS also provides full programmes related to the European integration process, usually contributed by associations of TV stations or by individual channels. These programmes may be used, free of charge by other broadcasters, on condition that the source is credited. Indeed the service as a whole is free of charge, and free of rights for non-commercial purposes such as news bulletins and information programmes.

EbS has in its eight years of operations proved the value of a free-to-air video picture agency promoting, literally, a vision of the European Union and all its works as it develops.

In the current state of media economics, the staple pictures of EU events that EbS provides probably make all the difference is many cases as to whether a European story is included in a bulletin or not. It has become an accepted partner for major media players. The channel has the technology to deliver its pictures quickly and accessibly, more recently by Internet as well. In a favourite Brussels buzz word, it has also created 'synergies' during its lifetime, prompting greater levels of co-operation between the information arms of the institutions, and more advanced planning in the interests of more complete and more comprehensive events coverage. In so doing, it has doubtless brought a little more general enlightenment to TV viewers about the complex and often distant story of 'Europe'.

The European Parliament and the Media
Jean-Charles Pierron

A well known French TV journalist interviewed recently about why his channel did not cover the European Parliament more replied: 'Be political and then you'll get coverage'.

In August 2003 the chief editor of a British television station expressed a quite different point of view:

> 'This is an important institution that many people think has increasing powers over decision making in Britain, and that – with the various Human Rights and other acts that have been passed – has increasing relevance actually to the way decisions are taken in this country.'

Is Great Britain unexpectedly europhile and France eurosceptic? Or is it a matter of how the media sees the Parliament?

The European Union and Television

Before examining media coverage of the European Parliament (EP) we need to know just what sort of media and what sort of programmes we are taking into consideration. I propose to look solely at European TV coverage and specifically within that news coverage[1], as well as the nature of relations between the EP, working journalists and those with wider editorial responsibility.

Television is the focus because – according to Eurobarometer No.59 (published in 2003) 59% prefer to get their news information from television while only 35% prefer daily newspaper, 23% radio, 19% by other publication and 15% by internet.

But at the same time citizens everywhere are asking for more information about the European Union, about its policies and its institutions. This is a priority – according to the Same Eurobarometer – for three out of four European citizens. Demand has risen 3 points since autumn 2002. Luxembourgers (88%), Swedes (86%), the Dutch (85%) and Greeks (84%) are the most avid for more information, but in every country a majority want to know more. Even in Britain, where only 59% want more information, these still far outnumber the 25% who say they do not want more.

Yet despite this strong demand for more information about Europe, supply still seems insufficient and inadequate.

In a recent study entitled 'Framing Europe: Television news and European integration' (Aksant Academic Publishers, Amsterdam 2003) Claes H de Vreese shows that European affairs account for only 1% to 2% of TV news in the UK and in the Netherlands, apart from summits and other exceptional European events.

A study by P. Norris in 2000 entitled 'A virtuous circle: Political communication in post-industrial societies' (CUP Cambridge) indicates a level of 2% to 3% for news devoted to Europe in all television news programmes. Norris suggests that 'the EU is peripheral in news coverage in the UK, Belgium, France, Italy, Germany and Spain, with only occasional peaks.'

A French study undertaken from September 2001 to May 2002 analysed news programmes over nine months on these same channels and found that Europe was the theme of only 64 programme hours in all, which came to an average of 7 minutes and 12 seconds per week on radio and 2 minutes 24 seconds on television.[2]

So there is clearly a big gap between the demands of viewers and the supply offered by television stations. The situation is similar in radio. It merits investigation.

The Nature of European News

According to editors it is the nature of European news which makes coverage difficult. On the basis of meetings and interviews with journalists and editors in many different countries, it is clear that covering Europe, and a fortiori the European Parliament, is seen as a challenge. Often the arguments put forwards are similar in all countries of the Union:

- The 'distance' between editor-in-chief at home in each country, the political editor and the corespondent(s) in Brussels does not help to promote a Europe story in the list of the day's news agenda. Correspondents also often cover both EU institution stories and news events across Europe, a fact which certainly does not make the job any easier. According to many journalists/correspondents it is often their editors who turn down European stories, while editors claim it is not they but the corespondents who determine the news agenda. One correspondent of a public service TV station put it like this: 'to get a story accepted you really have to harry your editors'.

- There is a mismatch between the European agenda and the national agenda that means decisions are taken in Brussels well before they are transposed into national laws. This time gap makes it hard for TV news with its desire for immediacy to treat this type of story.

- Reports, procedures and decisions at the European level are considered inaccessible and difficult to understand because of their high degree of specialisation. A French TV journalist described the European 'construction' as 'vague, complicated: you cannot easily see how to explain it'.

- Sometime the EU is seen as a separate world, an ivory tower where 'they' have their own language: Eurospeak. Another French journalist commented: 'To understand the European institutions you need a dictionary to hand all the time'.

- Frequently TV stations operate a form of self-censorship, assuming a lack of interest among viewers. According to a French journalist, 'we still have to attract the interest of viewers'. Sometime they assume a lack of knowledge among viewers as an excuse to kill a story, since viewers could not understand it anyway. (An odd conclusion given the Eurobarometer findings above.)

- And to deal with an EU story with clarity and rigour you need a good knowledge of the EU as a journalist. Broadcasters may also need time and tenacity, and in some cases – whether for lack of time or for laziness – it is just simpler and easier to select other items for the news agenda.

Selection Criteria

And yet some topics do get through the obstacle course and arrive successfully in the TV news. So what are the key conditions for being selected, for making it into the 'Top 10'?

For journalists and editors the criteria and conditions applied to any story which is proposed for TV news (and not just European stories) are in some respects universal.

- There has to be *conflict*. It may be a difference or disagreement between the national and the European level (Stability Pact, Alstom, for example), or between interest groups and the EU authorities or political parties (Pechiney, lorry drivers' demonstrations, cosmetic testing on animals), or between different political groups (for example on Social Policy) or even between different European Institutions (Parliament and Commission over the fate of the Santer team in 1999).
- There has to be some link to the *national or local* scene, preferably with economic consequences (GMOs, for instance).
- There has to be some *human-interest* element in the story (for example mammary implants).
- There has to be something *concrete or specific* which illustrates the impact of the issue or decision on everyday life.

You can go further – as de Vreese does in his study – and point to an *element of responsibility* (whose fault is it?) and an *element of morality* (for example, should a reference to Christian traditions be included in the European Constitution?)

And finally there is the issue of *differences* in the way different countries do things, differences of application and interpretation of these criteria between countries and between TV operators.

Parliaments and the Media

When you analyse carefully day-to-day business in the European Parliament you can find quite a large number of stories which merited (or could have merited) inclusion in TV news programmes. Many stories over the past twelve months have met the criteria listed above:

- European airspace and compensation for delays for passengers;
- Food security, especially GMOs and BSE;
- Environmental issues, especially waste management, renewable energy resources, drinking water standards, bathing water standards, noise pollution;
- Marine security, especially clear health warnings and bans on misleading publicity;
- Transport, especially the development of a European rail network;
- Liberalising the European electricity market.

For the editor-in-chief of one French radio network, the relevance of the list is self-evident:

> European topics, what are they? There is agriculture, environment, immigration, security, international trade, the economy, and food security: it is all managed by Europe. These are the subjects that people are interested in.

But the message is clearly not getting through everywhere. A study of French TV conducted in 2002 shows some thoroughly unsatisfactory results from Parliament's perspective. Media coverage of Parliament in French TV does not match the importance of its political role among the European institutions.

This study shows that only 21% of European news items analysed made specific reference to the EP, while 34% referred to the Commission and 16% to the European Council and the Council of Ministers.

Nonetheless, in certain circumstances and on a one-off basis (after 11 September, for instance, or on the election of a new President) Parliament can play a major role by leading the media agenda more strongly.

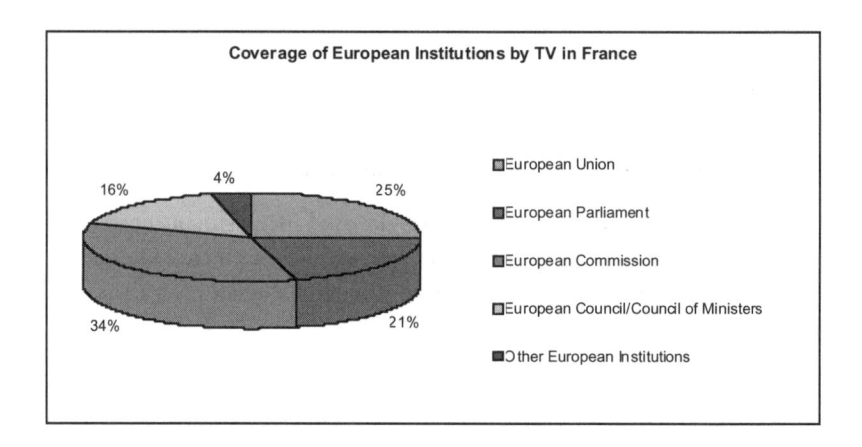

Coverage of European Institutions by TV in France

- European Union: 25%
- European Parliament: 21%
- European Commission: 34%
- European Council/Council of Ministers: 16%
- Other European Institutions: 4%

This explains why the EP, despite being quoted much less frequently than the Commission, is the subject of references which are on average longer than news about other institutions, and about the Commission in particular.

Thus a news item which mentions the European Parliament as 'principal institutional point of reference' for a European issue lasts on average for 2 minutes 28 seconds as against 1 minute 48 seconds for the Commission.

Over a period of eleven months the total duration of items in the study dealing with the EP was 819 minutes (more than 13 hours of programming), which was barely four hours less than the total time given over to the Commission.

During 2001/2002 the European Parliament took almost a quarter of the total transmission time devoted to the European institutions (23%). It managed this because it benefited from two factors which encouraged such journalistic treatment: a) its political configuration at the time, with a French MEP as President, and b) a series of particularly 'hot' items of international, European or French news.[3]

This study underlines Parliament's interest in alerting and informing journalists about news stories which may interest them, subject only to their subsequently deciding whether they want to run with them. They will have their own criteria and good reasons to follow up such stories, or not.

The audio-visual service of Parliament recently established a 'hotline' service for journalists to give them precisely this sort of help. An explanation follows in the next section.

Parliament and How Media Have Developed

Over the last twenty years the EP has devoted increasing attention to news transmitted by different media, in particular audio-visual media, which have become the prime forum for political debate.

According to the study by J.L. Missika,

- The rise of mass media, the 'depolitisation' of editorial offices in broadcasting, the end of the dominance of political parties and the emergence of a volatile electorate have all helped to push the prime focus for political debate towards the media.

- In this era of 'public democracy' electors no longer vote so much according to their political affiliation as depending on what is at stake at each election, and that changes each time. Voters decide what is at stake in a relatively homogenous manner on the basis of information from the same sources which are essentially neutral as far as party politics is concerned. Politicians are obliged to persuade the public on the merits of each issue and not simply on the basis of belonging to one ideology or another. Thus democratic debate is brought to the public though the media which constitute a new 'space' for discussion.

- This considerably modifies the obligations which politicians and parliaments are called on to meet. Parliaments in particular have to adapt to the constraints which apply in general terms to the media as a whole: the requirement to be *simple*, to be *accessible*, and to be *stage-managed*. They have to adapt also to constraints specific to television: to be *immediate*, to *demonstrate* and to offer *people* to give body to their activities.

Both politicians and institutions have to become *expert in communication* and to *adapt the constraints*, as well as adapting to them, in order to get themselves known, to be heard and to persuade.

- Now we are entering a new period in relations between parliament and the media. Internet, cable and satellite have revolutionised the traditional system of access to information by breaking the monopoly of professional journalists on primary sources of information.

- A limited number of political actors associated with big institutions now have the capacity to speak directly to the public (using internet or possibly television) without intermediaries or 'gatekeepers', and are able to give them detailed information regularly brought up-to-date.

- Big institutions have thus become not only a source for the media but media in their own right.

Transforming the audio-visual Landscape

At the beginning of the 1980s the audio-visual landscape was made up almost exclusively of public-service channels, few in number and in most member states enjoying a monopoly of TV broadcasting. Their requests for services from the audio-visual division of Parliament were limited to simple technical assistance. In a letter dated 20 January 1983 the President of Parliament wrote to the General Association of the Photographic and Film Press in Belgium specifying the tasks of Parliament's audio-visual division:

> 'The section TV is a unit for technical support, designed specifically for television services. The European Parliament has no intention of acting on its own in this area, but is on the contrary extremely open to the concerns of professionals in this field.'

Now there are hundreds of television channels in Europe. Many of them are commercial. In some countries there is a rough balance between public service and commercial stations; in others private channels have the lion's share of the audience.

This same period has witnessed the emergence of numerous regional and local TV stations. CIRCOM, the association or regional TV stations, now has over 350 members. The viewing figures for these channels are often very large. For instance, in France at peak viewing time, *France 3* reaches its largest audience which equals 45-50 per cent of potential viewers.

We should not overlook the creation and development of European satellite channels, another aspect of this media revolution. Some of them are well known and reach a considerable audience: *Europnews, BBC World, Deutsche Welle, TV5* and others. And very often the programme schedules of these stations offer a significant amount of European information.

In the near future the development of digital television and the link between TV and the Internet will create new media worth exploring and exploiting in the cause of greater public information.

Quite apart from technical issues, the economics of TV broadcasting have also been radically changed, in particular by the introduction of advertising, and fierce competition has developed in this market. Its effects in programming have been far-reaching, and many stations have moved to 24 hour broadcasting as a result.

This in turn has generated increased demand for pictures, which should – in principle – allow broadcasters to meet the strong demand from viewers for more information about Europe. But paradoxically, on major channels the space allotted overall for news has often been reduced, and the nature of the news broadcast has been seriously modified to the point that it resembles 'info-tainment'.

For the audio-visual division of Parliament these developments have altered the type and level of demand for its services. These have been considerably expanded. Technical assistance remains important; indeed, it has grown as the number of broadcasters has increased and as interest in Parliament has developed. Parliament has acquired new powers, especially as co-legislator with the Council on many dossiers which directly affect the citizen.

But quite apart from technical aspects, studies and enquiries show that journalists and their editors want more speedy information that is credible, clear and also pro-active, and which – through 'news alerts', personalised e-mails, telephone calls – is specifically suited to the needs and requests of the stations themselves. The audio-visual division's 'Hotline' service was created to respond to this expectation and this development. It is the latest service to be added to those offered to broadcasters by the division.

The European Parliament's Audio-Visual Division

The Audio-Visual Division of the European Parliament was set up in the 1970s with just two sections: photo and radio. The TV sector was added in 1982, following a decision by Parliament's Bureau from several years earlier (14 October 1976). In that same year *The Times* newspaper described the facilities that would be made available for TV journalists:

'The unit, of four television cameras and three videotape machines, will provide continuous coverage of the proceedings with studio and technical controls to permit television and radio stations in Europe to prepare their own reports for transmission in their own countries. Parliament would provide strictly technical services and editorial freedom would rest with journalists.'

At the beginning the main task of the Division was limited to covering the plenary debates of Parliament for the archives, followed by simple technical assistance to TV journalists from public-service broadcasters. Now the basic mission of the Division, within the framework of the information policy of Parliament, is to ensure the presence of the Institution on air and to promote the image of Parliament in the media.

The Division now offers TV and radio journalists a large range of services:

A. External Relations

This unit is responsible for relations with broadcasters, establishing and following up contact with different stations.

It has three main tasks:

- Accreditation and reception of journalists coming to Parliament to prepare programmes, offering assistance and practical information (special requests for filming, contact with specialist services of Parliament, etc.).
- Representation of the Division in various professional conferences and meetings organised in different European countries.
- Organisation of specialist seminars for journalists, editors and editors-in-chief from various TV broadcasters.

Since 2003, particular importance has been placed on the media needs of newly acceding states. Several meetings and visits have taken place and several broadcasters have sent correspondents to Brussels.

Some figures indicate the achievements of this unit to date:

- In 2002 over 1100 journalists were accredited at various sessions of Parliament, representing 466 TV channels.
- In 2003 the unit organised four seminars and attended congresses or conferences or visited TV stations on ten occasions.

B. The Hotline

The Hotline (the most recent unit) aims at providing assistance to broadcast professionals in their search of relevant information for news coverage or TV programmes about Europe.

- The *Hotline* offers specific information to assist and help journalists without interfering in their editorial choice.
- The *Hotline* brings up news that matters within the national and European agenda. It will highlight a European topic, which will have an impact on the national domestic agenda.
- The *Hotline* alerts media professionals via the telephone or e-mail when unexpected issues occur linked with the European and national agenda.
- The *Hotline* has no intention to compete with existing sources of information such as news agencies or EU correspondents. The *Hotline* offers another valuable complementary 'tool' providing professionals with a wider choice and a better understanding of EP's work.

Within one month of being set up, the Hotline was meeting with a positive response form journalists. By way of illustration, here is a message received in October 2003:

> 'The Hotline called me twice on the phone; it was really very 'cool'. They explained how I could research the story by country, by political group and so on. Then they even sent me a new list in alphabetical order, and all the contacts I needed. The Hotline seems a really good idea. In short, an excellent service. Many thanks.'

C. Technical Support

Currently the technical support facilities offered by the Division are as follows:

- ENG Crews - On average three crews, consisting of a cameraman and sound technician with Betacam SP or SX equipment, are available for use by broadcasters. On busy days we work with up to 5 crews working with our own material.
- Editing - Strasbourg and Brussels facilities allow cut-cut editing in several edit suites with editor. The formats we can handle are Beta SP, Beta SX and Digi Beta. Soon a new virtual server based editing system will be operational in Brussels.

- Transmission - Strasbourg has three outgoing lines, of which one is dedicated to EBU, one to SERTE/Globecast and one to either one of these. We also have an incoming facility for use in the studio.

  Brussels has one direct outgoing line to the EBU circuits. We will soon have our own incoming line as well as an additional outgoing line through a private company.

- Studio /Stand-up - Both the Strasbourg and Brussels studios come fully equipped and staffed for programmes up to a 1+4 set-up. Backgrounds can be natural blue and/or black with use of plasma screens and light effects, or completely virtual with blue-key. For down the line interviews our stand-up studio facility is available at the heart of the Parliament.

- Recording /Copying - Every plenary session has been recorded since 1983. Copies can be obtained on beta SP, SX or DVC PRO format. The sessions and other events like press conferences and important committee meetings are not only available on tape but also broadcast live on EbS for use free of rights by all broadcasters.

- Archives – The TV archives (12,000 hours) can not only provide footage of the parliamentary sessions; our video library also contains footage of committee meetings, press conferences and other events taking place in the premises of the European Parliament, plus thousands of hours of illustrative footage and location pictures.

- Result - Technical support services have been used increasingly over the years. In 2002, for instance,

    - 611 TV channels used such support (125 in 1993);
    - 6705 hours of support were used (2443 in 1993);
    - 1666 programmes or reports were made using Parliament's technical supports (672 in 1993);
    - 905 hours of TV were transmitted (388 in 1993);
    - 1424 radio pieces were made using Parliament's technical support (405 in 1993).

D. *Europe by Satellite*

Europe by Satellite (EbS) is the televisual press agency of the European Union. EbS transmits pictures and sound of news about the EU institutions to broadcasters on a daily basis. These items (news, live relays, stockshots, kits and dossiers) are copyright free and can be freely used by TV stations.

EbS has 12 channels for sound and can thus transmit simultaneously in the eleven official languages of the EU.

And the footprint of the satellite goes well beyond the area of the Union, as far as the edge of Eastern Europe and to North Africa.

For the Parliament, EbS is a vital service at the disposition of journalists, television stations and agencies. The aim of EbS is to make the day-to-day workings of the European Institutions accessible to all media without distinction in an open digital satellite signal.

Parliament features in EbS schedules in the following ways:

- *Live relays*: All plenary sessions (in Strasbourg and Brussels) are broadcast direct in eleven languages by EbS, which represents roughly 440 hours per year. Added to that are selected meetings of important committees and public auditions of candidates for the highest offices. That all TV stations in Europe have the chance to follow in real time all the plenary sessions of Parliament is an important demonstration of democratic openness.

  These live relays from Parliament represent about half of all live relays from all European institutions on EbS.

  In addition to the daily relay when Parliament is in session, EbS also transmits a résumé of the day's debates in the early evening.

- *News items*: Each day EbS transmits several 'news' stories, each lasting a few minutes. These items summarise or underline the most important items on Parliament's agenda, and they vary in number from one to six or eight when there are several important meetings being held.

- *Info clips*: These short dossiers of variable length are made up of illustrative pictures and informative facts on topics which are expected on Parliament's agenda in the coming week.

In total, Parliament took up 570 hours of EbS transmission time in 2002.

Many TV stations still prefer to make their own reports (sometimes with the EP's technical support), since this allows them to emphasise a specific angle, illustrated with interviews specific to that channel. EbS is complementary to that, and by its nature it will never be in a position to supply specific stories, but it makes the job of the TV journalist easier, letting him/ her concentrate more time on their own production.

Europe, Parliaments and the Media

The following table and chart summarise EbS activity in 2002.

EbS Transmissions 2002

	EbS Subjects	EVN EUN	Info clips	Video Stock shots	Long Summary	Subjects	Directs Hemicycle Strasbourg	Directs Hemicycle Brussels	Directs Convention Brussels	Live Press Conference	Recorded Press Conference
January	35	9	1			3:00:54	19:55:00			5:21:00	0:00:00
February	44	9		1	3	6:18:25	25:59:00	8:00:00	3:00:00	6:21:00	8:39:00
March	43	13	3		3	6:09:54	22:49:00	4:00:00	7:30:00	2:21:00	11:53:30
April	46	18	3		2	5:58:06	22:21:00	8:00:00	7:30:00	1:30:00	9:28:10
May	38	10	2		2	4:10:12	23:15:00		7:30:00	1:58:00	7:20:00
June	39	6	4		2	5:10:52	23:11:00	7:30:00	17:00:00	3:12:00	3:03:00
July	30	8	1	1	2	5:24:15	21:40:00		19:45:00	2:08:00	3:32:00
August	1					0:03:03			0:00:00	0:30:00
September	21	2	1		1	2:08:08			8:15:00	6:15:00	0:00:00
September I	11	2	2		1	1:08:57	21:53:00			0:30:00	0:19:00
September II	13	3	2		1	1:45:16	16:05:00			3:40:00	0:27:00
October	35	12	5		3	5:24:30	18:14:00	3:30:00	16:00:00	2:02:00	8:40:00
November	49	7	1		3	4:02:12	22:00:00	8:00:00	7:30:00	1:20:00	9:02:00
December	45	3	5		5	6:21:24	14:51:00	7:00:00	14:30:00	1:18:00	6:45:00
Total subjects	450	102	28	2	29						
Total time						57:06	252:13	46:00	108:30	31:41	75:53

Total time 2002: 57:06:08   571:23

180

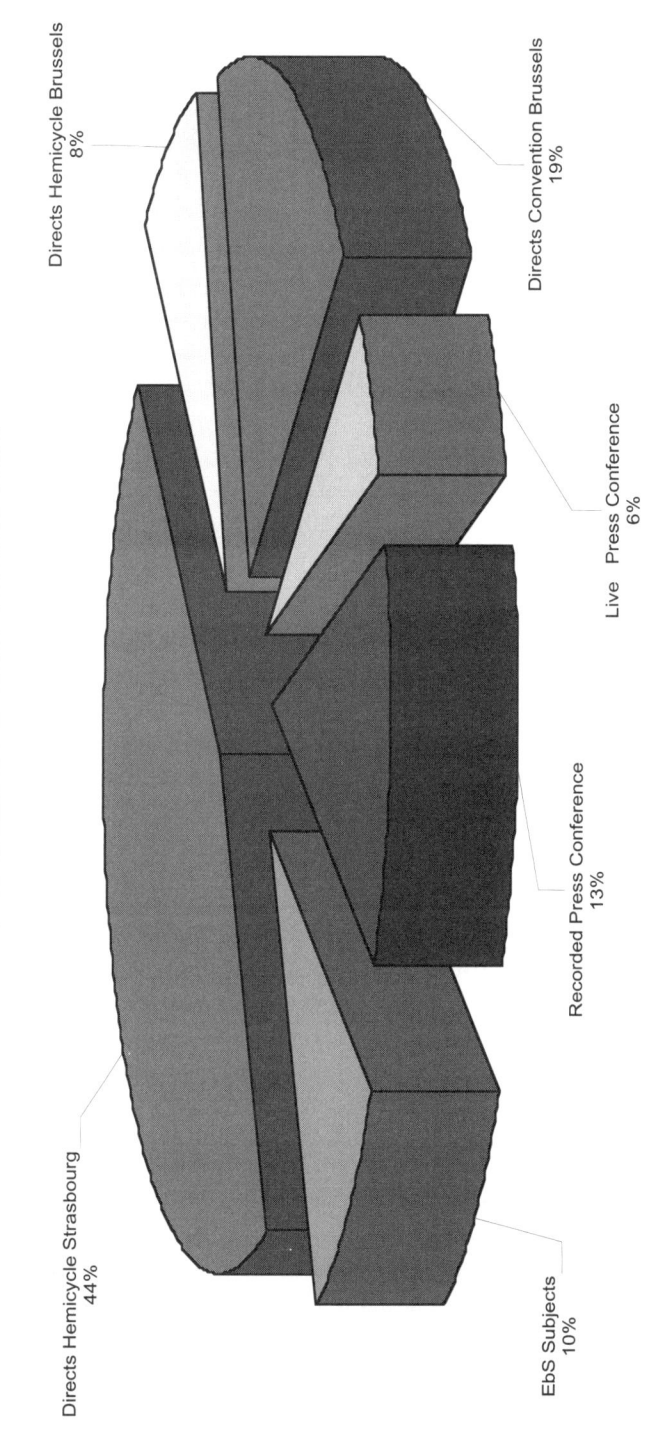

EbS Transmissions 2002

- Directs Hemicycle Brussels 8%
- Directs Convention Brussels 19%
- Live Press Conference 6%
- Recorded Press Conference 13%
- EbS Subjects 10%
- Directs Hemicycle Strasbourg 44%

E. Production

The production unit is responsible for programmes co-produced with other channels,[4] in particular *Euronews*, and regional and parliamentary channels.

Collaboration with Euronews and Parlamento

Euronews is the sole example of a paneuropean multilingual information/ news channel. *Euronews* operates as a public service TV channel in the EU partly because of its origins, partly because of public bodies owning its shares.

Since its inception in 1993 *Euronews*' new bulletins and specialist magazine programmes have regularly covered the work of the European institutions. Its coverage of the Parliament over recent years has taken different forms:

- A Euronews journalist, with technical support from the audio-visual Division in Strasbourg and Brussels during plenary sessions, produces short reports for inclusion in the stations news bulletins (every half-hour) and in the daily programme 'Europa'.

- Euronews covers the work of parliamentary committees on the basis of pictures and 'news' items transmitted by EbS, edited into news items for inclusion in Euronews bulletins.

- Euronews covers meetings of the European Council and broadcasts the press conference of the President of the European Parliament.

- Euronews also covers official visits and important travels by parliamentary delegations to third countries.

- Since 1994 Euronews co-produces a weekly magazine programme with the Parliament called 'Parlamento'. The audio-visual Division supplies technical support for this programme, which lasts eight minutes. Each week 'Parlamento' is produced by a journalist of a different nationality, matching the multilingual nature of Euronews, which transmits currently in seven languages: German, Spanish, Italian, Portuguese, French, English and Russian.

- The purpose of 'Parlamento' is to report and interpret the work of the European Parliament, the topics treated being a function both of Parliament's agenda and Euronews' own requirements in the light of its other magazine programmes and the current European news agenda.

Regional TV stations and Eurinfo

For over six years Parliament has paid particular attention to regional television which has the advantage of being close to the citizen. In most of the member states various forms of collaboration have been put in place, and the following table serves as an example of programmes produced and transmitted by regional ITV stations in Britain between May and September 2003.

Channels	May 2003	June 03	July 03	September 03
Tyne Tees	0	0	0	3
Granada	2	3	2	1
Yorkshire Tv	0	1	1	1
Grampian	1	1	0	0
STV	1	3	0	1
HTV WALES	1	4	0	3
CENTRAL	1	3	1	0
UTV	0	1	0	0
MERIDIAN	0	2	0	2
ANGLIA	0	1	0	0
CARLTON WEST	1	2	2	2
	7	21	6	13
TOTAL	**47 PIECES**			

A further important element of regional collaboration is the co-production of EURINFO, an 8-minute magazine programme, between the audio-visual Division and various local and regional TV stations.

EURINFO is transmitted by more than 60 stations and reaches a potential audience of more than 8,300,000 viewers in France, Belgium, Germany, Austria, Sweden, Italy and Portugal. It reaches a regular audience of approximately 4,000,000 viewers, and from 2003 it is being transmitted as well in Poland, Hungary and the Czech Republic.

Some TV stations – *Citizen TV, Canal 8 Le Mans, BHTV* – have responded positively to the idea of producing their own magazine programme based on EURINFO and linking the European and the local level, essentially by running local interviews and themes addressed by EURINFO. For some of these local and regional stations, EURINFO is sometimes the only European programming that they carry.

Parliamentary Channels and Demos

In 2000 the European Parliament set us a network of parliamentary channels in Europe. The participating channels co-produce a monthly exchange programme entitled 'Demos.'

The Network includes

- BBC Parliament (UK): part of the BBC, this channel is independent of the legislature but concentrates on live transmissions of debates especially from the House of Commons. The channel does not produce documentaries or similar programmes but does offer 'talk-shows' about European affairs, such as 'Politique'. This show is 30 minutes long and is recorded each week in Brussels or Strasbourg. It also broadcasts on BBC World. Since many MEPs speak English, it can draw on a wide range of politicians to take part.

- Bundestag TV (Germany): this channel is still under development following a decision by to legislature itself which wants its parliamentary sessions to be seen by a wider audience.

- Canal Parliament (Portugal): the channel of the Portuguese parliament.

- Canal Parliamentario (Spain): this channel is run by the press service of the Congress of Deputies in Madrid. Since April 2000 it has re-transmitted 'Demos'.

- Chamber TV (Luxembourg): this channel is the result of a decision by the Luxembourg Parliament to set up a station dedicated to political programming.

- Hellenic Parliament TV (Greece): this channel relays the plenary sessions of the Greek Parliament.

- LEP-AN (France): this is a private station set up in March 2000 and financed by the National Assembly. It shares a cable channel and satellite transponder with the equivalent organisation in the second chamber, Public Senat. It is a fully fledged TV station with own production (features and news) and an editorial staff of twenty journalists. LEP-AN produces a monthly magazine programme 'Vivre en Europe' presented by Alex Taylor, and – together with Public Senat – regularly relayed live debates from the sessions of the European Convention.

- Phoenix (Germany): created in 1997 as a joint venture by ARD and ZDF. It is a channel as much for political information in the broadest sense as for simply parliamentary news. The channel carries debates from the Bundestag and Bundesrat but not in their entirety.

- Public Senat (France): this is a private station set up in March 2000, the 'twin' of LEP-AN. The Chairman of the station is a well-known French journalist, Jean-Pierre Elkabbach, former Chairman of France Televisions. Public Senate produces a weekly magazine programme (52 minutes) called 'Paroles d' Europe'. It has also developed programming recently with short programmes on the Euro and other issues relating to European society, as well as visual biographies of MEPs from various states of the Union.

The channel regularly takes the EbS signal to relay live debates from the European Parliament and recently from the European Convention. It collaborates with LEP-AN on special projects from time to time.

- RAI TSP (Italy): part of the RAI public service network, RAI TSP has access to RAI transmitters for its output, which is principally short reports and extracts from EP sessions. RAI TSP also produces weekly magazine programmes 'Giorni d' Europa' (20 minutes) and 'Speciale Europa' (25 minutes).

The Italian Chamber of Deputies is currently considering setting up a specific parliamentary channel.

- SVT 24 (Sweden): a new public service TV with schedules covering news, sport and politics, SVT 24 is interested in Carrying 'Demos'.

- C-SPAN (United States) The Network also collaborates with C-SPAN in the USA and with C-PAC in Canada. C-SPAN is the original parliamentary channel, set up over twenty years ago to relay Congressional debates via cable to a wide audience. It is now well established in the broadcasting landscape of the USA, where viewers turn to CNN for international coverage and to C-SPAN for domestic political coverage. While the bulk of its programming is relays of debates in the House of Representatives and the Senate and press conferences by politicians, it has enlarged its production to cover interviews, short features, local debates and even book reviews, Co-operation with the European channels has developed in the framework of the network co-ordinated by the EP.

C-PAC in Canada looked to C-SPAN as its model, with the interesting variant of being a bilingual channel, English/ French.

Currently C-PAC is enlarging its production in order to establish itself as the leading political channel in Canada, with explanatory programmes, debates and analysis of political events.

The 'Demos' Exchange Programme

BBC Parliament Channel, Canal Parliamentario, LCP-AN, Phoenix, Public Senat and the Audio-Visual Division of the European Parliament all participate in the exchange programme.

'Demos' as a programme demonstrates all the richness, the variety of approaches and the difficulties of co-ordination of any network of TV channels. It is an exchange programme which has been in existence since January 2002, each channel sending an extract from a national debate or a brief report (4 minutes) to the European Parliament's Audio-Visual Division. The extracts are assembled at the European Parliament, the scripts translated into the necessary languages and the final programme sent to each channel for 'localisation' and end use.

Each channel has adopted 'demos' to its own identity and style of broadcasting. For example, BBC Parliament TV simply transmits extracts while LCP-AN and Public Senat create a studio-based programme and call on journalists or experts to 'decode' and explain information within the programme. The French stations prefer to translate debates and reports (voiceover), BBC Parliament prefers subtitling with original sound.

In the near future programmes produced by the parliamentary channels will have new possibilities for transmission offered by the Internet. By web streaming they will be able to establish an interactive dialogue between the institution and the viewer/user, the citizen.

In addition, the Audio-Visual Division of the European Parliament works closely with a number of non-European channels, chief among them CNN. It also pursues numerous TV co-productions as well as promoting Parliament through radio and photography. New initiatives are plentiful, especially through the activity of Parliament's offices in the member states and the accession states, and audio-visual work will be particularly important in the run-up to the European elections in June 2004.

All in all there is ample evidence of Parliament's desire to ensure a strong and effective flow of information and to nurture a dialogue between the Institution and the citizen through the professional media.

Conclusions
- On the one hand there is a strong demand for information expressed by different publics in Europe.
- On the other hand the media, while not shunning their responsibility, point out that Europe is a complex story, difficult to understand, 'slippery' and not particularly visual.

- And Parliament itself, ready to do what it can to help the media, while respecting the different roles of each, to report and to put into accessible form the day-to-day political story of Europe.

So what is it that still prevents all these elements combining to ensure a stronger presence of Europe on our TV screens? What needs to be done, and by whom?

- Journalists should not be made responsible for the present situation. For sure they should be better trained and better informed about the Institutions on which they are reporting, but it is not their job to promote the European Union. It is up to them to analyse as rigorously as possible what they learn and to report as clearly as possible on the life and work of the Institutions.

- As for the Institutions themselves, over and above showing goodwill and making facilities available, they should perhaps adapt their procedures and their language to make them more easily comprehensible by the media and by public opinion. This implies some simplification and an element of 'stage management' for debates and other activities so as to adapt them to the demands of radio and television.

Once these conditions are mest you could expect a notable improvement and increase in European information on television. But we should not be excessively naive or over-optimistic. There is at times a gap between good intentions shown in polls and enquiries and the realities of everyday life, subject to economic and other constraints. All too often it is the latter which condition the final choice.

But it is the Parliament, given its special role in the Union, which can encourage the right conditions to attract the interest and hold the attention of the media. It can do this with an information policy which is even more imaginative and bold than it has pursued so far. Then the media will produce news and information which meet the expectations of citizens and viewers throughout Europe.

Notes

[1] Most statistics in this article concern France and the UK. Other equally meaningful examples could have been drawn from comparisons with German, Spanish, Italian, Greek or other TV channels.

[2] Findings confirmed by Claes H de Vereese in his study 'Framing Europe' (p77).

[3] J. L. Missika, *Study for European Parliament* (2002).

[4] Collaboration with the Franco-German cultural channel ARTE has developed considerably following the creation of ARTE-INFO.

Media and Mobilization in the 1999 European Parliamentary Election
Susan A. Banducci and Holli Semetko

Introduction

In pluralistic democracies the press is often referred to as a 'watchdog' performing an oversight function and ensuring that the public holds elected officials accountable. More recently, the news media have been referred to as a political institution – 'an increasingly important and autonomous force in politics, independent of political parties' (Schudson 2002). The link between public debate and media coverage in European affairs has been considered in scholarly literature. Indeed, the popular backlash against Maastricht and the ratification crisis were attributed, at least in part, to a lack of public engagement and popular debate about integration (Baun 1996). Some have taken the perspective that the EU suffers from a communication deficit because the Commission and other institutions have failed to present to the public adequately the tasks they undertake (Meyer 1999). In other words, greater public debate and communication through the media could play an important role in legitimizing the EU. One implication from this line of reasoning is that if only the media paid more attention to the EU and its institutions, European citizens would learn to value it more.

Twenty years after the first elections to the European Parliament most Europeans chose not to vote in the parliamentary elections held in June 1999. These figures are down about six per cent from the 1994 elections and much lower than turnout in national elections.

But do these figures reflect public attitudes towards European integration? Are they suggestive of an apathetic, disinterested public largely negative about the latest developments in the European integration process? There has been much discussion and research about what can account for the low turnout in EU-wide elections, turnout that is much lower even than participation in local elections. Compared to national elections, European elections are considered to be 'second order' affairs. Voters do not think the European elections matter much, or are not given reasons to think they matter much, and thus they are less likely to show up on polling day (Reif and Schmitt 1980, van der Eijk and Franklin 1996). From this point of view, any positive turnout in European elections is viewed essentially as a product of institutional features such as compulsory voting, weekend voting and concurrent elections. However, others acknowledge that positive attitudes toward Europe play a crucial role in getting voters to the polling place (Blondel, Sinnott and Svennson 1998). Therefore, from that point of view the post-Maastricht decline in EU support may also have led to a decline in turnout.

Whether citizens fail to vote because European elections are not as important as national elections or because they harbor negative views about the EU, one might expect that media coverage during the election campaign could work to either increase awareness of the salience of the elections or improve attitudes about the EU. One of the few studies to examine the impact of media coverage on European elections (Blumler et al. 1983) - also the subject of this chapter - shows that turnout in the 1979 European parliamentary elections was higher in countries in which there appeared to be more active campaigns. Some have also cited the invisibility of the EP in the news and the negative tone in coverage of the EU as contributing factors to negative attitudes and low participation (Norris 2000). In this chapter, we examine three factors relating media to turnout in European elections: (1) changes in national media systems since the first European parliamentary campaign; (2) the content of news coverage during the 1999 European parliamentary election campaign; (3) the relationship between visibility of the campaign and turnout.

Media Systems

One of the most dramatic developments since 1979, the year of the first European parliamentary election, has been the widespread change in Europe's national media systems. State funded public service monopolies came to an end in most countries by the early 1990s. Currently, in most EU member states, the information environment is fragmented, competitive and commercialized. In other words, any study that examines the relationship between news media, how citizens learn about the EU and whether they participate in European elections must first examine how the media environment, where most people receive information about the EU, has developed since the first European election. The decline in public service broadcasting, transition to dual systems of broadcasting, change in the audiences for traditional media and the depoliticization of the press have coincided with a period of deepening European integration (see Semetko, de Vreese and Peter 2000). Characteristics of the media system, such as public financing, cross-media ownership, newspaper partisanship, journalistic traditions, and policies regulating political content in media all have an impact on public affairs programming and news and information content. The media environment will determine to some extent the role that the media play in an election. Access to information by the mass of people - and the mass of voters in particular - differs enormously according to the national context. The type, amount and access to information will be decided by a variety of factors that are related to the media system and political regulation of the media. Below we discuss how growing commercialization and changes in audiences have altered the information environments where citizens get information about European affairs.

Most European countries, for example, have a strong tradition of state or public ownership of broadcasting. France only legalized private broadcasting in the 1980s and the prohibition against commercial broadcasters in Austria did not change until the late 1990s. Almost all countries demand some form of statutory regulation of broadcasting, as a way of ensuring pluralism over the airwaves. Also the degree to which regulation is carried out through independent commissions or by parties in government varies across countries. Although there has been increasing deregulation at the national level, there have been several attempts to regulate at the EU level. Proposals by the European Parliament, however, to prevent media concentration and cross-ownership have largely been ignored by the Commission. Specifically requirements at the national level in relation to media campaigns during election periods, the regulation of broadcasting frequencies, content quotas, and fairness in coverage have a significant influence on how broadcasters discharge their responsibilities at election time.

In the early 1980s the public broadcasting model dominated all EU countries (except Luxembourg which has always had a private broadcasting system): compared to the 40 public channels available in the early 1980s, there were only 4 commercial stations (Brants and de Bens 2000). Currently, with the exceptions of Austria and Ireland, most countries can be considered dual broadcasting systems with similar numbers of private and commercial stations and similar audience reach on the commercial and private channels. The shift to dual systems has meant changes in the way broadcasting is financed, the accountability mechanisms and the mix of programs available to viewers. These consequences of the changes in public broadcasting have influenced the ability of the media to facilitate and mobilize voters at election time.

Table 1: Changes in National Media Systems in EU Member States

	1980	1990	2000
Public Monopoly/Govt. Funded	Belgium, Denmark, Sweden		
Public Monopoly/Mixed revenue	Austria, Finland, France, Germany, Greece, Ireland, Netherlands, Portugal, Switzerland	Austria, Denmark, Ireland, Netherlands, Portugal	Austria
Private Monopoly/Advertising revenue only	Luxembourg (4)	Luxembourg	Luxembourg
Dual System	Italy, UK	Belgium, Finland, France, Germany, Greece, Italy, Spain, Sweden, UK	Belgium, Denmark, Finland, France, Germany, Greece, Ireland, Italy, Netherlands, Portugal, Spain, Sweden, UK

Source: Brants and de Bens (2000) and Siune and Hulten (1998) updated by authors with data from the European Audiovisual Observatory (2002).

Table 1 shows the transition in media systems from around the time of the first European Parliamentary election in 1979 to the latest election in 1999. During the first EP election, the majority of countries were public monopolies and now virtually all EU member states are operating under dual broadcasting systems. In 1980, Luxembourg was the only country to have a commercial broadcast channel operating. While Italy and the UK allowed commercial broadcasting, no commercial channel reached over 50 per cent of the households. Currently, all countries, except Austria, have a national terrestrial commercial channel that reaches at least 50 per cent of households. Indeed, the number of commercial stations and their reach has increased substantially since 1980.

The table also shows the shifts in the revenue models for public television broadcasters. There are two models of funding for public service broadcasting. First, public service broadcasting can be financed solely by government either through the collection of a license fee paid by television viewers or from general revenue resources from the government budget. Currently no European PSB operates solely through government or collection of license fees. The closest to this pure model of government funding is the BBC. While most resources come from license fees, the BBC also collects approximately 15 per cent of its revenue from the sale of programs. Advertising contributes only a minimal amount to the financing of Swedish public broadcasting. The second model of public broadcasting financing combines advertising revenue with some form of government funding (license fee or direct transfers from the budget).

There are several consequences of the increasing commercialization of broadcasting for voters and the ability to gather information to make electoral choices. First, there is increasing diversity in viewing choices. More channels translates to more total airtime which increases the diversity of choices for viewers. While there is more choice for viewers, as they turn to different channels there is less commonly shared information or experience. This process has been referred to as audience fragmentation. Second, information that citizens are exposed to may be changing. With more channels, there is greater competition for audiences and public broadcasters must be concerned about maintaining their base of viewers. The assumption is that with the addition of commercial stations there has been an increase in entertainment programming and that public channels have responded to this by also offering more entertaining choices and increasing the entertainment value of news programs. However, all things considered, there has tended to be a general increase in the amount of political information available and no concrete evidence that there has been a 'dumbing down' of the political information on public channels (Brants and de Bens 2000). Increasing choices for viewers may mean, however, that less attention is paid to news.

With the introduction of commercial channels there has been a decline in audiences for public service broadcasting channels. Table 2 shows the decline in audiences across most in EU member states. The table shows only the change from 1992 to 1999 which is a shorter time period than that displayed in Table 1. Therefore, we only see the possible effects of the growing commercialization of channels during the last ten year period. Despite the shorter time span, there are substantial shifts in the audiences for public channels. The largest declines have occurred in countries that had the most dramatic shifts in the media systems between 1990 and 2000. For example, the market share for *Canal 1* in Portugal dropped by over 30 per cent between 1992 and 1999. During this same period, two channels reaching a majority of households were introduced in Portugal. *ORF* in Austria also suffered a significant shift in market share. While no commercial channels were introduced, terrestrial commercials channels from Germany now take up a considerable amount of the market in Austria. With very few exceptions, market shares are declining across all public channels, in most cases in favour of commercial stations. These commercial stations are comprised of terrestrial, cable and satellite channels. The shares of these stations is growing as well as, in some cases such as Spain, the market shares for regional channels.

Table 2: Change in Market Shares of Public Service Broadcasting Corporations

		Market Shares		
		1992	1999	% Change
Austria	ORF1	41	24.4	-16.6
	ORF2	32	33.1	1.1
Belgium/Flemish	TV1	25.5	22.6	-2.9
Belgium/French	RTBF1 (la Une)	15.2	17.2	2
Germany	ARD1	21.7	14.2	-7.5
	ZDF	21.3	13.2	-8.1
Denmark	DR TV 1/2	34.7	30.7	-4
	TV2	40.3	36.1	-4.2
Spain	TVE-1 (RTVE)	32.4	24.9	-7.5
	TVE-2/La 2	13.1	8.1	-5
Finland	TV1(YLE)	30	23	-7
	TV2 (YLE)	19	20	1
France	France 2	24	22.3	-1.7
	France 3	13.6	16.3	2.7
UK	BBC1	33.7	28.4	-5.3
	BBC2	10.5	10.8	0.3
Greece	ET-1 (ERT)	11.3	5.6	-5.7
	ET-2/NET (ERT)	6.4	3.9	-2.5
Ireland	RTE-1 (RTE)	36	31.9	-4.1
	Network 2 (RTE)	21	19	-2
Italy	RAIUno	18.9	22.8	3.9
	RAIDue	18.2	15.7	-2.5
Netherlands	Ned-1	14.8	11.2	-3.6
	Ned-2	15.1	16.3	1.2
	Ned-3	14.3	9	-5.3
Portugal	Canal 1 (RTP)	61.5	27	-34.5
	TV2 (RTP)	17.6	5.6	-12
Sweden	Kanal-1 (SVT)	30	21.4	-8.6
	TV-2 (SVT)	26	25.8	-0.2
				-4.8

Source: European Audiovisual Observatory 1995 and 2002

Besides shrinking audiences for public television where the mission is to provide educational and informational programming, there is a concern that public broadcasting, in order to compete with commercial stations, is changing its programming to provide more entertaining and attractive programs to keep audiences interested. There are two claims being made in this argument. First, that public broadcasting normally provides more information in its programming. Second, over time the informational content on public broadcasting has declined. If audiences' are moving away from public channels where there is less news and information content, citizens will be receiving less current affairs programming. Therefore, changes in audiences viewing habits and changes in the media system most likely serve to reduce the ability of the media to facilitate participation in the electoral process.

While the number of public broadcasting viewers has been declining, another important source of information has also been on the decline. Newspaper readership has steadily been declining across all European countries. In most countries, newspaper readership has either declined or at best remained stable. The decline of the partisan press has also meant a weakening of traditional ties between readers and their newspaper. Also, stable newspaper readers tend to be leaving the national press for local newspapers (Gustafsson and Weibull 1997). Table 3 shows the patterns of reported newspaper readership between 1980 and 2001. These estimates are based on the number of persons in Euro-barometer surveys who say they read a newspaper everyday. Based on these data, there are two countries where there has been an increase of over 5 per cent in the number of people saying they read a newspaper everyday – The Netherlands and the former Western part of Germany. In some other countries, readership has stayed stable (less than a 5 per cent shift) and in other countries such as Greece, Denmark, Luxembourg, Austria and the United Kingdom, there has been a more substantial decline. It is clear that in most countries, the ability for the press to facilitate electoral participation is declining if citizens are turning away from newspapers as a source of information.

Table 3: Changes in Newspaper Readership

	Newspaper Readership % who read a newspaper every day				Change 1980-
	1980	1986	1995	2001	2001
FRANCE	31.9	28.4	30.2	25.7	-6.2
BELGIUM	38.1	28.4	33.8	29.5	-8.6
NETHERLANDS	51.7	42.6	62.9	60.3	8.6
GERMANY-WEST	46.1	60.4	57.6	59.7	13.6
ITALY	27.6	25.2	31.0	30.0	2.4
LUXEMBOURG	70.0	41.0	63.5	55.8	-14.2
DENMARK	67.5	63.1	56.2	53.0	-14.5
IRELAND	45.5	38.0	44.5	45.8	0.3
GREAT BRITAIN	57.7	51.3	57.9	46.7	-11.0
GREECE		43.0	20.9	13.5	-29.5
SPAIN		21.0	27.9	24.0	3.0
PORTUGAL		14.6	14.2	19.6	5.0
GERMANY-EAST			66.8	56.0	-10.8
FINLAND			72.2	66.4	-5.8
SWEDEN			70.0	68.2	-1.8
AUSTRIA			72.4	54.0	-18.4

Sources: Euro-barometer: EB13, EB26, EB43.1, 55.1 (EU member countries only available at time of survey).

Overall, changes in the media systems both in terms of the increasing diversity of channels from which to choose and the changing viewing and reading patterns of the audience suggest that the ability of the media to facilitate voting is not as strong as it was at the first European parliamentary election.

News Coverage during the 1999 European Parliamentary Election Campaign

While there have been significant changes in the media systems, little is known about how these changes influence the actual content of the news or how specifically European news is covered. To date there have only been a few studies that rely on content data to analyze how European Union affairs are reported in various media: Blumler (1983), Leroy and Siune (1994), Kevin (1999) and Norris (2000) are the most significant. The European Institute for the Media is also working on European Parliament coverage.

These published findings reflect a focus on both media effects on opinion and variation in coverage across countries. Some conclusions, from Blumler's edited volume on the 1979 EP elections, show that the campaigns differed significantly in each country and media coverage tended to produce separate issue agendas in each country. However, some generalizations across the nine countries could be drawn. First, journalists tend to rely on the same sources. Second, voters across all countries tended to tune into television as their main source for election news. Third, social demographic characteristics were related to election media use across countries. Fourth, the EP election was not a highly salient event in any country.

A similar study was conducted around the 1999 European parliamentary elections. Two news programs in each country for the two weeks prior to the election were examined for their coverage of the election campaign. The news programs were chosen because they were the most widely watched news programs in the countries concerned. The news programs were also selected on the basis of public or commercial status; one public service news broadcast and one commercial news broadcast were selected. The exceptions to this were Ireland and Austria where only one news broadcast was chosen because no secondary news program existed. In Belgium four news stations (comprising both public and commercial stations) and in Greece three programs were selected.

A short technical note is in order here to explain that, while only one news program was selected each day, the study assumes that similar news coverage occurred on the station's other news broadcasts. This assumption becomes important when merging the content data with the survey data. In some countries, rather than asking which news broadcast a respondent regularly watched, only the station was asked. For example, in Greece whether a respondent watched Mega news, ET1 news and/or Antenna news is recorded in the study, while the 19.55 broadcast on Antenna and the 20.00 broadcast on Mega is coded in the content analysis.

In order to examine the mobilizing impact of television news coverage, we have created indicators of visibility of the EP elections in the news. The measures are calculated for each outlet. For the two week period prior to the election, both the proportion of the stories and the proportion of time covering the EP elections was calculated. Only in a few countries is the proportion of time substantially different from the proportion of stories. These differences seem to be due to variations in the structure of news coverage in different countries.

Figure 1 shows the visibility of the campaign on television news according to the number of stories that mention the EP election. The table is arranged to show the differences between coverage on public and commercial news outlets. The campaign was most visible in Greece. Depending on whether the percentage of stories or the percentage of time is considered, over 20 per cent of the time of the evening news broadcasts on the main public channels in this country was devoted to stories that made some mention of the EP election. However, the campaign was not as visible on the commercial stations in Greece as on public TV. Indeed the EP campaign overall was more visible on public news programs. The campaign was least visible on stations in Belgium, the Netherlands, Spain, Germany and the U.K. With the exception of Spain, this low visibility was largely true of the commercial stations in these countries as well as of public broadcasters. However, the public station news in Finland devoted considerably more time to the EP campaign than did the commercial station. The visibility of the EP campaign on Finnish commercial broadcasting ranks among the countries with the lowest visibility.

In a comprehensive analysis of variations of the 1999 campaign visibility, Peter (2003, 47) demonstrates that there were a number of factors related to the prominence of European election coverage. Some factors were related to the actual outlet while other factors were related to the country in which the news broadcast occurred. Public broadcasters were significantly more likely to give the EP election more coverage. This fits with the expectation that public service broadcasting provides more informative content. Member states which had been members of the EU for longer and had experienced more EP elections also tended to have lower visibility. The nature of elite opinion on the integration issue also affected the visibility of the campaign. There was more coverage in countries where elite opinion was polarized on the issue of European integration. News values research leads one to expect that news stories that contain conflict will be more newsworthy

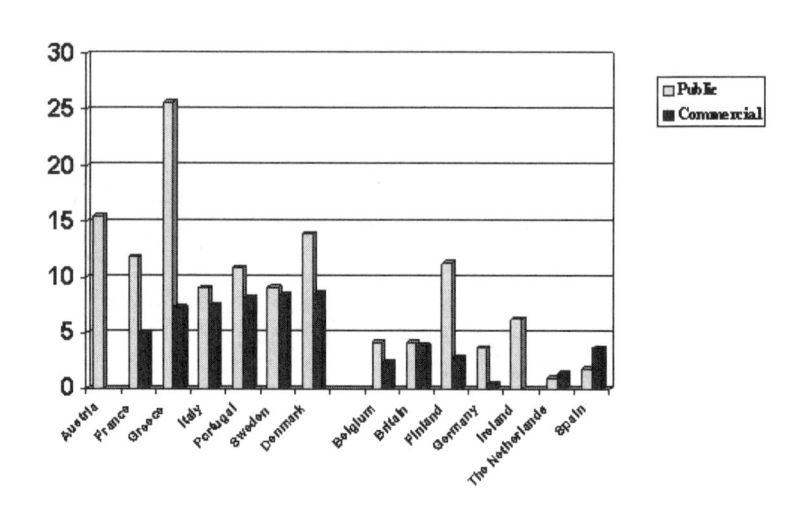

Figure 1: Visiblity of EP Campaign on TV

Chart displays the percentage of stories (excluding weather and sports stories) that mention the EP elections.

and gain greater coverage. News editors were likely to cite the lack of newsworthiness of EP elections as a reason why they chose not to cover them (see de Vreese 2003). Other factors such as concurrent elections in Belgium, Ireland and Spain are also most likely related to lower levels of visibility of the EP campaign in these countries.

Figure 2 shows similar data for the quality press in each country. Only front pages of the listed newspapers were coded for the two weeks prior to the EP election. This measure of visibility thus also takes into account the prominence of the campaign in these newspapers. The Flemish *De Standard* contained no front page stories that mentioned the election campaign. The French language *La Libre Belgique* also carried relatively few stories that mentioned that EP campaign. There was some overlap between countries that had low visibility on television news and those countries that had low visibility on the front page of the quality press – Belgium, the Netherlands, Germany and the UK. Greece and Portugal on the other hand had relatively higher levels of campaign visibility in newspapers as was the case also with their television news.

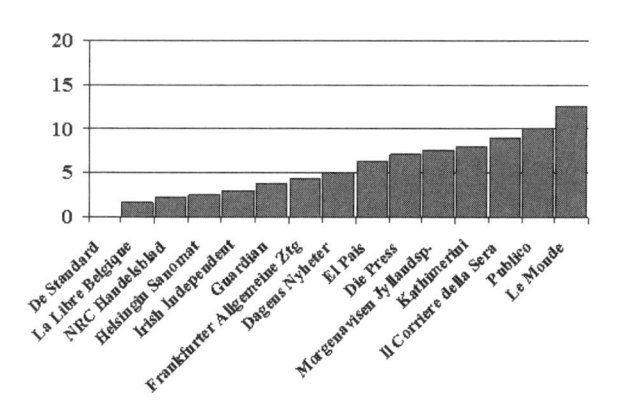

Figure 2. Visibility of EP Campaign on Front Page of Newspapers

Chart displays the percentage of stories that mention the EP elections.

Media and Turnout

The key question is how the visibility of the campaign on television news influences turnout in an election. As a campaign becomes more visible, the cost of obtaining information is lowered and voters are more likely to perceive the election as important. Our research found a positive relationship between visibility and turnout (r=.14). In general, and as you might expect, as visibility increases turnout also tends to increase. However, as was evident from our research, other factors also influence turnout. Compulsory voting in Belgium obviously kept turnout high in the European election even though the campaign had low visibility in the news. Other countries such as Ireland and Spain held concurrent elections with the European elections. Turnout in Spain was above 60 per cent but the visibility of the European campaign was low, suggesting that turnout was boosted by holding the European election concurrently with domestic elections. The 'downside' however is the possible conclusion that holding concurrent elections may tend to boost turnout but at the expense of the European campaign being covered less fully in the news.

Conclusions

In this chapter we were primarily concerned with describing the media systems in the EU member states, the structural changes in these systems that have taken place since the first EP election in 1979, and how these structural features are related to the content of news coverage. We are also interested in how visibility of the EP campaign in the news can mobilize voters. We see that viewers have more choices in terms of media outlets and this may alter the amount of information they receive about politics and the EU in general, and about EP elections specifically. Changes in the media environment are also related to changes in the relationship between citizens and the traditional media. Citizens are watching less public television and reading fewer newspapers, both of which factors lower the probability of their being exposed to political information. In the first EP election, more people would have been likely to see the one or two public channels that were carrying news coverage of the election or to have read a newspaper that mentioned it. In the most recent election, however, the diversity of commercial stations has led to a fragmented audience, certainly in respect to political information, and a decline in newspaper readership has reduced the potential for an informed electorate.

We were also interested in establishing the extent to which campaign visibility in the news actually matters when it came to individuals' decisions to vote in the 1999 EP elections, an election in which turnout reached all time lows in many countries. Previous research on turnout in EU elections has emphasized contextual influences such as compulsory and Sunday voting, as well as support for the EU, as important variables for predicting turnout. But little has been said about the relative influence of these variables in comparison with campaign news variables and media use variables in the context of EP elections. Despite the gaps in knowledge about specific relationships between these variables, we do see, however, that increased media coverage does have the potential to increase turnout in European elections.

References

Blumler, Jay G. (ed.).1983. *Communicating to Voters: Television in the First European Parliamentary Election* (London:Sage).

Brants, Kees and Els de Bens. 2000. 'The Status of TV Broadcasting in Europe' in Jan Wieten, Graham Murdock and Peter Dahlgren (eds.) *Television across Europe*. (London: Sage) pp. 7-22.

Eijk, Cees van der and Mark Franklin (eds.) 1996. *Choosing Europe? The European Electorate and National Politics in the Face of Union*. Ann Arbor: University of Michigan Press.

Kevin, Deirdre. 1999. 'The Sphere of Debate for European Parliament Election Campaigns: How European media outlets reflect a transnational event?' The Bulletin (European Institute for the Media) 16:30-32.

Leroy, P and K. Siune. 1994. 'The Role of Television in European Elections – The Cases of Belgium and Denmark,' *European Journal of Communication* 9:47-69.

Norris, Pippa. 2000. 'Blaming the Messenger? Political Communications and Turnout in EU Elections.' In Citizen Participation in European Politics. Demokratiutredningens skrift nr 32. Stockholm: Statens Offentliga Utredningar.

Reif, Karlheinz and Hermann Schmitt. 1980. 'Nine Second Order National Elections: A Conceptual Framework for the Analysis of European Election Results', *European Journal of Political Research* 8: 3-44.

Siune, Karen and Olof Hulten. 2000. 'Does Public Broadcasting Have a Future?' in Denis McQuail and Karen Siune (eds.) *Media Policy: Convergence, Concentration and Commerce* (London:Sage).

*The authors acknowledge the support of the Amsterdam School of Communications Research – ASCOR and the European Union's Fifth Framework Programme for assistance in collecting the data used in this report.

Notes on contributors

Dr Susan A. Banducci is Director of Research, Earl Survey Research Lab and Assistant Professor, Political Science Department at Texas Tech University. Prior to that she was Senior Research Fellow. Institute for Governance Studies, University of Amsterdam, The Netherlands and Research Fellow. Amsterdam School of Communications Research.

Olivier Basnée is a French academic researcher and journalist who recently reported from Brussels.

Dr Martyn Bond is a former European civil servant who has also reported from Brussels and Strasbourg for the BBC. He is a visiting Professor of European Politics and Policy at Royal Holloway, University of London, Director of the London Press Club and a former Director of the Federal Trust.

Dr Jean K. Chalaby is Senior Lecturer in the Department of Sociology at City University, London. He has written extensively on the impact of broadcast technology on European society.

Professor Stephen Coleman is Cisco Professor of e-Democracy at the Oxford Internet Institute and a fellow of Jesus College, Oxford.

Jim Dougall is Head of the European Commission Representation in the United Kingdom and a former BBC correspondent.

Lars Hoffmann is pursuing academic research at Oxford having recently worked on the European Constitution project for the Federal Trust.

Professor David Morgan is emeritus Professor of Mass Communications at the University of Leeds and author of The European Parliament. Mass Media and the Search for Power and

Influence. (Ashgate 1999). He has also contributed numerous articles on related subjects to the European Journal of Communication and the British Journalism Review.

Bridie Nathanson is a Brussels-based consultant on e-governance strategies.

Anthony O'Donnell is Head of Audiovisual Production Services at the European Commission. He was formerly Head of Production in the Audiovisual Division of the European Parliament, and prior to that a BBC journalist and Production Manager at VisNews.

Roy Perry is a Conservative MEP, first elected in 1994 and again in 1999. He is a Member of the Committee on Culture, Youth, Education, the Media and Sport, and a former Senior Lecturer in Politics.

Jean-Charles Pierron is Head of the Audio-Visual Division of the European Parliament.

Stewart Purvis is the CEO of Independent Television News which until recently held a 49% shareholding in Euronews.

Professor Holli Semetko is Vice-Provost of the Emory University at Atlanta, Georgia and Director of the Halle Institute for Global Learning at the same university. From 1995 until the summer 2003, she was the Chair of Audience and Public Opinion Research on the Faculty of Social and Behavioural Sciences at the University of Amsterdam (UvA), The Netherlands.

Norbert Schwaiger is a former European civil servant who for many years was responsible for the press office and media relations of the General Secretariat of the Council of Ministers in Brussels.